How to use Company REFS

A GUIDE TO INVESTING WITH
REALLY ESSENTIAL FINANCIAL STATISTICS

How to use

A GUIDE TO INVESTING WITH REALLY ESSENTIAL FINANCIAL STATISTICS

by

Jim Slater

A HEMMINGTON SCOTT PUBLICATION

Second Edition, December 1994

First published in Great Britain in 1994 by
Hemmington Scott Publishing Ltd.
City Innovation Centre
26-31 Whiskin Street
London EC1R 0BP

ISBN 0 9512632 34

Printed and bound in Great Britain by
Butler & Tanner Ltd, Frome and London

Design: Matthew Waites & Associates, Dana Kidson,
Stephen Matthews, Debbie Charlton

WARNING

All entries and tables in *Company REFS* are based on factual information extracted from sources believed to be reliable and do not constitute any investment advice or investment advertisement. Neither the publisher nor the author accept any responsibility and expressly disclaim liability for any errors, omissions or mis-statements.

Stock market investments, and the income from them, can go down as well as up. They may also have poor marketability. When you seek advice, also ask about marketability. The shares referred to in the text of this guide book are for illustrative purposes only and are not an invitation to deal in them. Neither the publisher nor the author accept any responsibility for the contents of the guide book, which is not a substitute for professional advice.

Readers should seek professional advice from and conduct their investment activity through an appropriately authorised person.

CONTENTS

ACKNOWLEDGEMENTS

In July 1993, when Peter Scott and I agreed to go ahead with *Company REFS*, neither of us realised that it would take so long to bring to the market. Marc Pullen and his team of analysts have worked with great exactitude, persistence and determination. The product of all our labours is far more comprehensive than we at first envisaged and it will continue to be improved and developed over the next few years.

I would like to put on record my gratitude to the entire management and staff of Hemmington Scott for their unflagging enthusiasm and dedicated hard work on the REFS project over the last 15 months. In particular, for helping with this guide book, I would like to thank Peter Scott for his clear thinking, tenacity and editorial help. I would also like to thank Chris Cole for his excellent Technical Appendix and for editing all of my work.

Tom Stevenson of the *Independent* has also edited the guide book and has made many suggestions for improving the text and structure of most of the chapters and the Technical Appendix. Thanks are also due to Nicolee Stevens for helping to design the guide book and prepare it for publication.

As always, I would like to thank my long-suffering secretary, Pam Hall, who has typed the drafts of *Company REFS* innumerable times. I would also like to take this opportunity of thanking God for word processors.

PREFACE

When I first met Peter Scott of Hemmington Scott, the publishers, we discussed the idea of producing a monthly book updating the key financial statistics and ratios that are used by professional investors. I suggested including only those statistics that are really useful, and proposed that we name the publication *Really Useful Financial Statistics*. Fortunately, Andrew Lloyd Webber had beaten us to it by naming his company *The Really Useful Company*. I say 'fortunately' because the new name, *Really Essential Financial Statistics*, says exactly what it means and is more easily remembered by the attractive mnemonic - REFS.

The words 'Really Essential' were not chosen lightly. I wanted the company entries to give investors every statistic necessary to value a share. They had to include, to name but a few, return on capital employed, price-earnings ratio, growth rate, price-earnings growth factor, price-to-sales ratio, the trend of margins, directors' dealings, a graph of relative strength and earnings per share, the position of the share in its index, the consensus of brokers' estimates, earnings per share on an FRS3, IIMR headline and normalised basis, borrowings and cash flow. All the available space is taken up by essential statistics like these, so there is no room for anything superfluous. You know when you look at any figure in *Company REFS* that it is there for good reason and will be a positive help to you in valuing a share.

Company REFS is divided into two volumes:

THE COMPANIES VOLUME

Detailed individual entries for all UK quoted and USM companies, excluding investment trusts, giving a huge range of statistical information.

THE TABLES VOLUME

1. Over 40 pages of tables highlighting key statistics every month. These include, for example, lists of the companies in each of the indices with the highest return on capital employed, the highest and lowest price-earnings ratios, the highest and lowest dividend yields and the candidates for demotion and promotion.

2. Sector listings and tables with comparative statistics.

3. Additional price-sensitive and relevant information including:-
   a) A schedule of directors' dealings over the last six months.
   b) A list of Chief Executive Officer changes during the last 12 months.
   c) A list of all company profit and dividend announcements, including interims, quarterlies and preliminary headline numbers.
   d) A list of revisions of consensus forecast changes.
   e) A list of all warrants and convertibles.

To explain *Company REFS*, I will begin with a simple outline of the elements of a typical entry in the Companies Volume showing what the various initials stand for, how each statistic is calculated and the way it should be used. I will follow this with a guide to the Tables Volume.

Finally, I will give some practical examples of how to use *Company REFS*. They are hypothetical and do not constitute investment advice.

In the Technical Appendix, you will find a full and detailed explanation of how each *Company REFS* statistic is calculated.

TO HELP READERS FULLY UNDERSTAND THE COMPANY ENTRIES, THERE IS A FOLD-OUT COLOUR KEY AT THE BACK OF THIS BOOK.

1

THE KEY STATISTICS

At the top right-hand side of each company entry is a shaded panel like this one:

PRICE (NMS 5) 26-SEP-94	985p T
norm eps (pr)	59.5p
market cap	£314m
turnover (94AR)[9]	£298m
pretax (94AR)	£42.4m

			m	s
DY (pr)	%	2.45		
PER (pr)	x	16.7		
PEG (pr)	f	1.00		
GR (pr)	%	16.5		
PCF	x	15.0		
PSR	x	1.00		
PRR	x	26.5		
PBV	x	4.16		
PTBV	x	4.26		
GEAR	%	–1.77		
MARGIN	%	13.6		
ROCE	%	21.9		

FT-SE Mid 250	192nd
market overall	292th

The panel is highlighted to catch your eye because the figures in it give you an instant fix on the company in question. They include key statistics to enable you to decide whether or not the company is of immediate investment interest.

PRICE

Price

The price taken is the mid-market close on the latest possible day before going to press; this will normally be the Monday before publication and the date will always be given.

Price

When a rights issue is in progress, the shares are suspended or a company has made or received a takeover bid, the letters R, S or T will appear to the right of the price. The date and nature of the event are also shown as the last item in the ACTIVITIES/OUTLOOK panel under the graph.

The symbol NMS in the bracket means normal market size. It gives an idea of the share's liquidity by showing the average trading quantity for the stock. NMS Bands are in thousands with a lowest level of 500 and a highest of 200,000. *Company REFS* shows these two levels as .5 and 200 respectively and always takes off the last three noughts. For example, 'NMS 5' indicates an average market trade of between 3751 and 6667 shares.

In May 1994, the complete table of NMS Band levels was as follows:

NMS Band	REFS figure	Share Equivalent	No. of SEAQ Securities
500	0.5	0 - 667	960
1000	1	668 - 1,333	321
2000	2	1,334 - 2,400	214
3000	3	2,401 - 3,750	159
5000	5	3,751 - 6,667	158
10,000	10	6,668 - 12,000	135
15,000	15	12,001 - 18,000	61
25,000	25	18,001 - 33,000	74
50,000	50	33,001 - 60,000	53
75,000	75	60,001 - 93,000	12
100,000	100	93,001 - 160,000	9
200,000	200	more than 160,000	2

The share equivalent column indicates the range represented by each NMS band. The fourth column shows the number of stocks in each band.

NORMALISED EARNINGS PER SHARE (norm eps)

Norm eps

The most important feature of the EPS entry in *Company REFS* is that it is not a reported figure but, where possible, a rolling 12-month view of expected earnings over the next year. Because of this, it changes every month and gives a dynamic, up-to-date view of a company's future profitability.

Whenever future estimates are available, *Company REFS* focuses on the 12 months immediately ahead and this is indicated by the letters in brackets 'pr' (denoting prospective). If no forecast is available, historic figures based on the last reported 12 months results are used.

The prospective normalised EPS figure is calculated by apportioning brokers' consensus forecasts for the current and next financial periods. For example, if the calculation were made on 1st March 1994, for a company with a financial year ending on 30th June 1994, a third (four months) of the consensus estimate for the current year would be added to two-thirds (eight months) of the estimate for the following year ending 30th June 1995.

The 12-months ahead method of calculation used in *Company REFS* has three important advantages:-

1. The company entries and tables are always as *up-to-date* and dynamic as possible.

2. The figures in the tables are always as *comparable* as possible.

3. The figures in the tables (and the company entries) are *smoothed* to avoid violent swings in ranking in the tables on the day results are announced.

In response to the introduction of Financial Reporting Standard 3, several different versions of EPS have evolved. The most useful of these,

Norm eps

from an investor's point of view, is normalised EPS, which has been adopted by *Company REFS* in the key statistics panel.

You will find in Chapter 3 a fuller explanation of normalised EPS and the process carried out by *Company REFS* (and many brokers) in determining the adjustments that are usually made to the FRS3 reported earnings figures. The key differences are that normalised EPS exclude exceptional items and possess three important characteristics:-

1. They reflect the underlying *trading* performance of the company.

2. They can be used as a *measure* of performance against expectations.

3. They clarify the *historic record of the operating performance* of a company.

The main limitation of normalised EPS is that they reflect the results achieved during an accounting period when a company had a certain structure, which may have changed. For example, normalised earnings include the results of trading businesses which have been discontinued or sold and only part of the results of businesses acquired during the year.

Market Cap

MARKET CAPITALISATION (market cap)

The 'market capitalisation' of a company is calculated by multiplying the market price of its ordinary shares by the number in issue. It gives an instant idea of the size and substance of a company.

Over the last thirty years, companies with small market capitalisations have outperformed those with higher ones. As I say in my book, *The Zulu Principle*, - 'elephants don't gallop.' This point is demonstrated by a

Market cap

graph comparing the Hoare Govett Smaller Company Index to the FT All-Share Index.

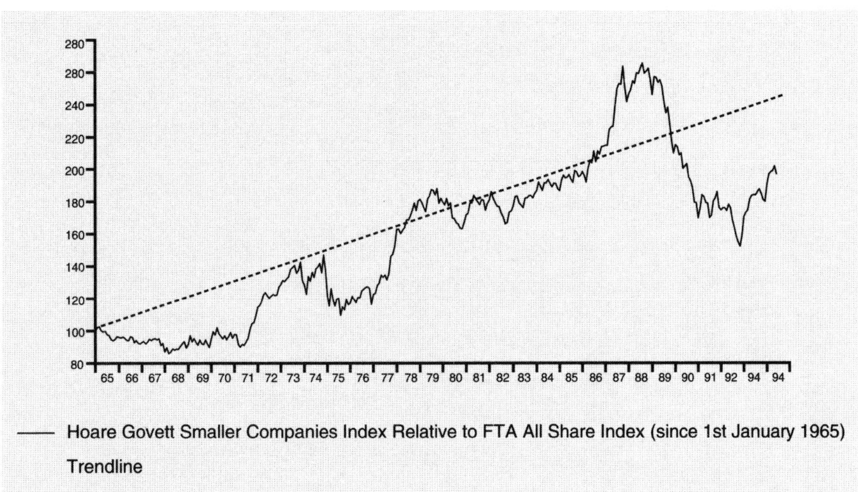

During the years 1989 - 1992, small companies have performed less well than the market as a whole, so they are now below their trend line and appear to have scope for catching up in 1994.

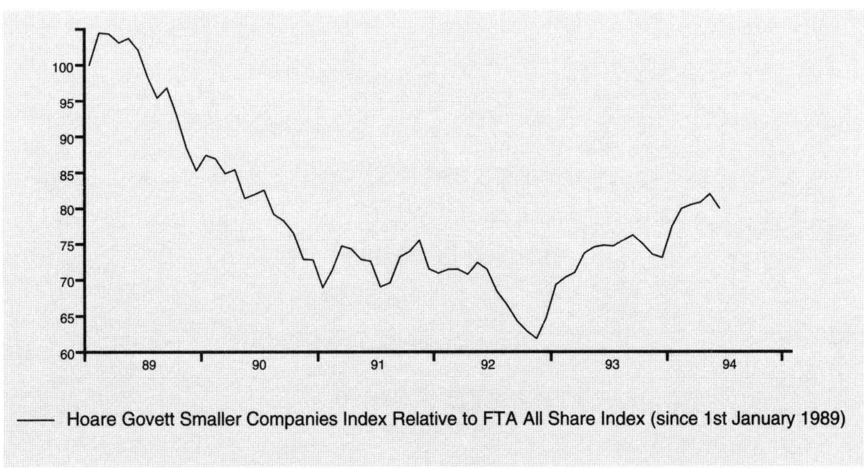

The compensating advantage of larger companies is that they tend to be safer and the marketability of their shares is far greater. For this reason many institutions avoid small capitalisation stocks.

Turnover

TURNOVER

Turnover is the total sales (excluding VAT) of a company as shown by the last annual report (AR) or by the announcement of the preliminary results (PA) for the following year.

Turnover gives an immediate indication of the size and stature of a company.

Pre-tax

PRE-TAX PROFITS

Pre-tax profits are the total profits of a company before tax as shown by the last reported accounts (AR) or by the preliminary results (PA) for the following year.

DY

DIVIDEND YIELD (DY)

The dividend yield is an important investment tool. There is very strong evidence to suppport the argument that high-yield portfolios outperform the market as a whole:-

1. During the 20 years from 1973 to 1993, £1000 invested in the average UK Growth unit trust, with dividends reinvested, grew to £12,800; in the UK General sector the comparable figure was £14,989 and in Equity Income £16,856. The best growth fund grew to £23,435, the best general fund £24,927 and the best income fund £28,232 (figures by Micropal).

2. Michael O'Higgins' book, *Beating the Dow*, clearly demonstrates that, on a total return basis, high yielding stocks beat the

American market as a whole. One of O'Higgins' systems simply selects the ten highest-yielding Dow stocks. At the end of each year he repeats the whole exercise again, selling those companies that no longer measure up and replacing them with new high-yielders.

O'Higgins' statistics show that, by following this system over a period of 18 ½ years from 1973 to 1991, an investor would have enjoyed an average annual gain of 16.61% compared with only 10.43% on the Dow. The ten stock portfolio outperformed the Dow 13 times out of 19. After adding dividends received, but with no charge for commissions, the cumulative gain before tax was more than 1750% against only 560% on the Dow.

3. Capel-Cure Myers, in an excellent paper dated March 1991, reviewed the extensive work of a Mr. M. Levis who had analysed about 4000 companies between January 1955 and December 1988. The results demonstrated that UK portfolios comprising low-yielding shares performed much worse than those containing some of the highest-yielding shares.

Mr. Levis also proved that, during the period, portfolios with an average yield 25% above the market average, as a general rule, substantially outperformed the FT All-Share Index. He also concluded that there was no evidence that portfolios containing high-yielding stocks were riskier in terms of their beta or their standard deviation of returns than their low-yielding counterparts.

High-yielding shares outperform the market on a total return basis because they are usually companies that are out of favour. The stockmarket over-reacts to good and bad news, often driving up the prices of growth shares to dizzy heights and leaving less popular (and apparently more risky) stocks to languish at bargain levels. In essence, therefore, buying high-yielding shares contains a strong element of contrary thinking.

Another reason high-yielding shares do well is advanced by O'Higgins. He points out that, historically, dividends have accounted for 40% - 50% of the total return on the Dow, so a higher annual payout represents a significant cumulative advantage to shareholders.

In the UK too, the 1994 BZW Equity-Gilt Study makes it clear that over 75 years dividends have accounted for about 42% of the nominal total return on equities. Because UK companies do not cut their dividends lightly, they are also a much firmer element of total return than share price growth based on potentially volatile earnings.

There is another possible reason for high-yielders being relatively strong performers. When analysts examine a share and assess its likely future value, say a year hence, not all of them factor into the equation the extra income that is likely to be received in hard cash and could be reinvested. In some cases, it is a significant factor which is only too easy to overlook.

The arguments for buying the shares of high-yielding companies are compelling. But it is worth pointing out that there is a definite cyclicality in buying high-yielding shares. In a climate of falling interest rates, they perform well as investors become more income-conscious. However, this can easily change.

It is a dangerous game to buy shares just because they appear to have a high yield. A high yield can indicate the market's concern that the dividend may be cut. To be selective, investors following a high-yield system should avoid companies with dividends that are very poorly covered or for other reasons seem likely to be reduced.

To help assess the risk of a dividend cut, a range of important factors are highlighted in other panels of each company entry: **DY**

1. *Dividend cover* - A dividend that is poorly covered is obviously more likely to be cut. A well-covered dividend is far more likely to be maintained or increased.

2. *Cash flow per share* - EPS provide cover for the dividend in terms of profits, but cash flow per share is a stronger test of future dividend-paying capacity.

3. *Gearing or net cash* - Companies with very high borrowings may have difficulty in paying dividends, even if they make substantial profits. Major creditors can press for repayment and balance sheets may need to be repaired before dividends can be freely paid.

Clearly a company with a strong dividend cover, high cash flow per share and net cash is unlikely to cut its dividend. Conversely, a company with poor dividend cover, weak cash flow and high gearing is very likely to do so.

To ensure that *Company REFS* is as up-to-date and active as possible, the dividend yield is based on the consensus of brokers' dividend estimates for the 12 months ahead. As with EPS, this is usually a combination of forecasts for the current and next financial years, apportioned on a pro-rata basis. For example, in the October issue of *Company REFS*, the yield for a company with a year ending 31st December includes three months of the consensus forecast for the current year and nine months of the following year's estimate.

When future estimates are available, this is indicated by the letters 'pr' in brackets and the dividend yield is based on the consensus of brokers'

DY

forecasts for the 12 months immediately ahead. If there is no forecast, historic figures based on the last reported 12 months results are used.

As already explained, the method of calculation used in *Company REFS* ensures that both the company entries and tables are as up-to-date and dynamic as possible. Also, the figures in the tables become directly comparable and are smoothed to avoid violent swings as results are announced.

The first stage of calculating the dividend yield is to add back the basic rate of tax (1993/94 - 20%), which has been deducted by the company. Assuming a 2.1p dividend, the calculation is as follows:-

$$\frac{2.1p \times 100}{80\ (100\text{-}20)} = 2.63p, \text{ which is the gross dividend}$$

The dividend yield is the gross dividend as a percentage of the share price. If the shares trade at 200p, the calculation is as follows:

$$\frac{2.63p \text{ (the gross dividend)}}{200p \text{ (the share price)}} \times 100 = 1.31\%$$

The first column of moons indicates the level of the dividend yield relative to the market as a whole and the second column relative to the company's sector. A full black moon shows a relatively high dividend yield and a blank moon a relatively low or non-existent one.

The tables in the Tables Volume list the 25 shares with the highest prospective dividend yields in each of the main FT indices and the 25 highest outside the indices.

PRICE-EARNINGS RATIO (PER)

PER

As an investment measure, the Price-Earnings Ratio (PER) is, in many ways, like a ranging shot. It gives an investor an instant fix on the kind of company that is under review and the market's expectations.

The PER is best used to measure how much an investor is being asked to pay for future earnings. A growth stock with a higher prospective PER than the market average clearly anticipates above average future earnings growth. Conversely, a growth stock with a low PER expects below average future performance.

Very high PERs are obviously dangerous. The slightest setback to expectations can cause a vicious downturn in the share price. In contrast, low PER stocks are relatively safe, although often uninspiring. Banks and utilities, for example, often trade on very low PERs.

Recovery stocks often command very high PERs at the bottom of their cycle when a substantial recovery is anticipated. At the top of the cycle, their PERs can then fall to below-average levels. Because of this, great care should be taken when comparing the PERs of companies in different sectors.

The weakness of the PER in isolation is that it does not tell you how much you are paying in relation to the estimated future growth in earnings. It is therefore a one-dimensional measure. For example, how much should be paid for a stock growing at 40% per annum compared with another growing at 20% per annum? The relationship between the PER and the growth rate makes the price earnings growth factor (PEG) a far more pertinent and effective measure.

Company REFS has focused upon the 12 months immediately ahead as the most dynamic and useful measure of a company's PER. As already explained, the prospective normalised EPS figure is calculated by apportioning estimates from the current and following financial periods.

PER

For example, if the calculation was made on 1st April 1994 for a company with a year ending on 30th June 1994, a quarter of the estimate for the current year would be added to three-quarters of the estimate for the year ending 30th June 1995. As the *Company REFS* prospective PER is based on the *prospective* normalised EPS figure, it will always cover the 12 months following the calculation date.

As already explained, the method of calculation used in *Company REFS* ensures that the company entries and tables are as up-to-date and dynamic as possible. Also, the figures in the tables become directly comparable and are smoothed to avoid violent swings as results are announced.

When future estimates are available, this is indicated by the letters 'pr' in brackets and the PER is based on the consensus forecast for the 12 months immediately ahead. If there is no forecast, historic figures based on the last reported 12 months results are used.

The PER is calculated by dividing the company's share price by its earnings per share (EPS). For example, if the share price of a company is 100p and its earnings per share are 5p, the PER is 20.

In May 1994, the average UK company had an historic PER of approximately 20 and, after forecast growth, a prospective PER of about 15. The forecast growth may seem to be substantial, but in fact a large element of it was anticipated recovery from previous setbacks as opposed to pure growth. Individual companies making up the market average of 15 had PERs ranging from 4 to over 100, but the vast majority were between 10 and 30.

The moons show the PER of a company relative to the market and then relative to its sector. The tables show the 25 stocks with the highest PERs and the 25 with the lowest in each of the indices and outside them.

PRICE-EARNINGS GROWTH FACTOR (PEG)

As we have seen, the PER of a company is of limited use as an investment tool because it only gives a one-dimensional measure of the price of a share relative to future earnings per share; it does not show if that price represents good or bad value.

The Price-Earnings Growth factor is a much more sophisticated measure because it relates the PER of a company to its future earnings growth rate and gives a better indication of value. Everyone knows that great growth shares merit a high PER, but the PEG helps you to determine how high and whether or not the shares are a buy or are losing touch with reality.

The PEG factor is calculated by dividing the prospective price-earnings ratio of a share by the estimated future growth rate in earnings per share. In May 1994, for example, the average *leading* UK growth share had a prospective multiple of 15 and was looking forward to increased year-ahead earnings growth of 13%. The average prospective PEG was therefore 1.15 (15/13). A low PEG value indicates that investors are paying a relatively low price for future earnings growth; a high PEG indicates that the shares are relatively more expensive.

A PEG below the average of 1.15 is superficially attractive, whereas a PEG of well above 1.15 would seem to be relatively expensive.

Over the long term, it has paid to buy the market on a PEG of one or below. Because of this, a company growing at 15% per annum would obviously be very appealing on a multiple of 15 or less. At a growth rate of 20% per annum, a multiple of 20 would also be very attractive.

Because the prospective PEG is a dynamic measure, it is always calculated by apportioning figures from the current and following financial periods using estimates in just the same way as for prospective PERs and normalised prospective EPS.

PEG

When a PEG is based on the consensus forecast for the next twelve months, this is indicated by the letters 'pr' in brackets. If there is no forecast, historic figures based on the last twelve months are used.

As already explained, the method of calculation used in *Company REFS* ensures that the company entries and tables are as up-to-date and dynamic as possible. It also ensures that the figures in the tables are directly comparable and are smoothed to avoid violent swings as results are announced.

How the PEG method works is best illustrated by the hypothetical example of a company growing at 25% per annum on a prospective multiple of 16. This would give a very attractive PEG of 0.64. When the forecast becomes a reality, and next year's projected growth of a further 25% becomes the focus of attention, the shares then enjoy a double benefit. First, from the higher earnings figure used in analysts' calculations and, second, from a change in the multiple as the market accepts that a higher PER is justified. At an early stage in the company's development, the multiple might rise from 16 to 20, so the earnings gain of 25% would be compounded by a further 25% increase from the status change, resulting in a total gain of 56.25%.

To illustrate the dramatic impact this can have on the share price, imagine that before the announcement of results, expected earnings of 10p per share and a PER of 16 implied a price of 160p. After the announcement, the higher PER of 20 on forecast earnings of 12.5p would result in a share price of 250p.

In addition to helping to maximise the upside potential from a share, the PEG can also be used as a defensive measure. A company with a below average PEG is obviously less vulnerable (all other things being equal) than a share with an above average PEG. It is therefore worthwhile periodically calculating the average PEG of a growth portfolio to evaluate how defensive it would be in a bearish climate.

There are a number of important caveats to bear in mind:-

PEG

1. The PEG factor is designed especially to measure growth stocks. It does not work well for recovery stocks, cyclicals and asset situations.

   Frequently, it is difficult to distinguish between recovery and growth. For the PEG measure to work at its best, the figures should be based on *sustainable* growth or the expectation of it.

   Coming out of a recession, almost all companies are recovering to a greater or lesser extent. However, those with a record of consistent growth over the previous four years are very different from companies which have suffered from a major setback and are trying to recover to their former profit levels.

   Company REFS has classified companies as growth stocks and awarded them a PEG *only* if they have at least four years of consecutive earnings per share growth. This can be either in the last four years if there is no forecast, or a combination of past growth (usually two years) and future forecast growth (usually the current year and the one ahead). The *Company REFS* approach is dynamic as it allows companies that are benefiting from a recent management change to qualify for a PEG. A quick visual impression can also be obtained from the graph, which clearly shows whether or not a company is a growth share under this definition.

2. A low PEG factor is, by itself, not a sufficient reason to buy a share. Although compromises are often necessary, the selected company should ideally have a competitive advantage, strong cash flow, insignificant debt and positive news-flow.

PEG

3. The PEG method of selecting growth stocks works at high levels of growth, but the dangers of high multiples are much greater. For example, a share growing *reliably* at 30% per annum would, in today's markets, merit a PER of at least 30. Growth at such a high rate is not, however, usually sustainable, so the downside risk is increased. The effects of a change in news-flow, even from excellent to reasonably good, could have a disastrous effect on a high-multiple stock (especially if it has no dividend yield).

   The PEG measure works at its best with companies which have earnings growing at 15% - 25% per annum, with PERs within five points either way of the average. Based on the average prospective multiple of 15, the best and safest results would be obtained with growth stocks with PERs in the 12 - 20 bracket.

4. PEGs are calculated on normalised earnings. The earnings forecasts are based on consensus figures obtained from a very large number of UK brokers. These figures are updated monthly, but the reliability of their consensus forecast (and therefore the PEG) is obviously much enhanced if there is a large number of brokers covering the company. The forecast is also more reliable if there is a small standard deviation. (The standard deviation indicates the extent of the deviation of individual estimates from the overall consensus figure).

5. Brokers' estimates of future EPS may be based on the assumption that the company will have a below-normal tax charge. In some cases it may enjoy this benefit for several years to come; in others EPS may suffer a setback as the tax charge rises to a normal level.

As with other investment criteria, the PEG cannot be considered in isolation. However, it is the single financial statistic that gives an instant fix on whether or not growth shares *appear* to be cheap or dear.

The column of moons shows the PEG relative to the market and the company's sector. A full black moon shows a relatively high PEG, a half-filled moon an average one and a blank moon a relatively low one. PEG

GROWTH RATE (GR%)

GR

The growth rate of a share is an important investment criterion, but obviously has to be related to the PER and the consistency and sustainability of the future earnings stream. If *Company REFS* has given a company a PEG, this means that there are at least four years of consecutive earnings growth made and/or forecast. The company can then be classified as a growth share and the growth rate becomes a much more meaningful figure.

When future estimates are available, these will be indicated by the letters 'pr' in brackets and growth rates will be based on the consensus forecast for the 12 months following the calculation date.

If no future estimates are available, the growth rate is based upon the average growth in historic normalised EPS over the last two years. However, if the growth in the second year is less than the first, the second and most recent year's EPS growth is used instead.

As with normalised EPS, PERs, PEGs and DYs, the growth rate is calculated by apportioning the figures from the current and following financial periods covered by estimates, the aim being to show the rate of growth for the 12 months immediately ahead.

PRICE-TO-CASH FLOW (PCF)

PCF

The PCF of a company indicates how much annual cash flow you are buying per share. A high PCF shows that cash flow is slim in relation to the share price. Conversely, a low PCF is usually very attractive. If the

PCF

PCF is much higher than the PER, the causes of the difference need to be established.

From an accounting point of view, a company's ability to pay investors an increasing flow of dividends is determined by its profitability. In practice, however, a more important measure of its financial health is its cash flow.

The PCF, in itself, does not indicate a strong cash flow; it simply tells you if the share price is high or low in relation to it.

A company's net cash flow has to fund the following:-

1. Repayment of any loans
2. Future capital expenditure
3. Dividends on ordinary shares.

Cash flow is a key measure of the capacity of a business to service these requirements, helping to highlight:-

a) If creative accounting has been at work. (This is determined by seeing if there is a major disparity between the trend of cash flow and EPS on an IIMR basis, i.e. excluding non-trading profits and losses).

b) If the future dividend is safe. Earnings are usually more volatile than cash flow and there is a greater relationship between cash flow and dividends than between cash flow and earnings.

c) Future liquidity and gearing. Cash flow is the raw material that will be used to pay off debts and improve liquidity. Without an adequate supply, gearing will increase and liquidity will deteriorate.

PCF

d) If a company has been over-trading. If earnings per share are expanding rapidly and cash flow is shrinking, this can indicate over-trading; for example, excessive funds may be locked up in growing debtors. This, in turn, raises the question of whether credit policy is too lax or if customers are unable to pay.

e) If future expansion plans and proposed future capital expenditure can be funded from within. This, in turn, is a kind of cross-check on the validity of a high PER based on expansion plans and capital expenditure.

Capital expenditure requires special attention. It is accepted as an appropriation as opposed to a charge against cash flow. However, in some cases capital expenditure is necessary for the continuance of a business (e.g. the replacement of old machines with new ones for the same purpose).

Capital expenditure on brand new machines for a new and additional factory is quite another matter. Unfortunately, it is not possible to distinguish readily between capital expenditure on expansion and on necessary replacement. Investors should, however, keep an eye on the level of capital expenditure each year and try to determine from broker and press comment how much of it is expansionary (as opposed to necessary replacement).

PCF is calculated by dividing a company's market capitalisation by its cash flow. However, there is a problem - there is no generally accepted way of calculating cash flow. One popular method was simply to add to profits those items requiring no cash outlay. The main one is, of course, depreciation. Also, for example, an adjustment would be made for the profit retained by an associate company that has been equity-accounted. The associate company's profits would be deducted from operating profits and be replaced by the dividend received in cash.

PCF

The Accounting Standards Board has a mandatory requirement for a Cash Flow Statement, which splits cash flow into different categories and attempts to classify sources of movements into their economic causes. Headings now include Net Cash Inflow from Operating Activities and, under FRS1, this figure must be reconciled with operating profits. Other than depreciation and associated company profits, the main additional items are increases and decreases in stocks, debtors and creditors. A typical reconciliation might be as follows:-

		£000
Operating profit		1000
Depreciation		100
Increase in stocks		(10)
Increase in creditors		50
Decrease in debtors		40
NET CASH INFLOW FROM OPERATING ACTIVITIES		1180
RETURNS ON INVESTMENTS AND SERVICING OF FINANCE		
Interest received	100	
Interest paid	(250)	
Interest element of finance lease rentals payment	(40)	
Dividends received from associated undertaking	60	
Dividends paid (excluding ordinary dividends)	(20)	
NET CASH OUTFLOW FROM RETURNS ON INVESTMENTS AND SERVICING OF FINANCE		(150)

PCF

TAXATION		
UK corporation tax paid	250	
Overseas tax paid	30	
		(280)
NET CASH FLOW		*750*

If the company's market capitalisation was £15.0m, this would mean that the PCF was $\frac{£15.0\text{m}}{£750{,}000} = 20$

PRICE-TO-SALES RATIO (PSR)

PSR

The PSR is an invaluable tool for spotting recovery situations, especially with companies that are making losses and are therefore in a kind of 'black hole'. When this happens, there is no PER and sometimes no dividend yield against which to value the shares. The PSR then comes into its own and provides a measure of a business's potential value, if and when it recovers. All other things being equal, a share with a low PSR is obviously better value than one with a higher ratio.

Needless to say, turnover is only valuable to a business if it can eventually be converted into profit. Contracting companies, for example, report very high turnover, but, except in building booms, rarely make much profit. Profit margins, the trend of margins and sector comparisons should, therefore, be studied in conjunction with PSR statistics. Sector comparisons often reveal interesting anomalies and investment opportunities in particular industries.

Another important and variable factor is the level of a company's debt. A company with no debt and a low PSR is clearly a better proposition than a company with very high debt and the same PSR. At some time

PSR

in the future, the debt will need to be repaid and further equity will almost certainly be issued. The extra shares then have to be added to the market capitalisation, increasing the PSR of the company in question.

It follows that gearing should be at reasonable levels to make PSR comparisons valid. Otherwise notional allowances need to be made to allow for the likely issue of further equity. The method of calculating the allowances would, of course, have to be consistent between the companies compared, but certainly the PSR should not be taken at its face value for a company that is very highly-geared.

Many investors are used to looking at the market capitalisation of a company against its sales and are used to referring to sales as being a number of times the market capitalisation. The PSR is the inverse of that ratio and is used to be consistent and to make comparisons more valid with the other ratios used in *Company REFS.*

The PSR is calculated by dividing the company's market capitalisation by its total sales, excluding VAT. This is the same as dividing the company's share price by the company's sales per share.

To take a simple example, in March 1991, Next had a market capitalisation, based on a price of 30p, of £100m and sales of £400m. The PSR was therefore a very attractive 0.25 - £100m/£400m, and it is no surprise that, with new management, by August 1994 the share price had recovered to 261p.

It is interesting to note that Next still had such a low PSR even after the sale of Grattan, when some kind of recovery was foreseeable. Prior to that, in December 1990, its market capitalisation had slumped to £24m against forecast sales, including Grattan, of £800m. The PSR was therefore an astonishingly attractive .03, although, at that stage, recovery was very difficult to foresee.

40% Special Discount!!

	Full	40% Discount
❑ UK Monthly	£795	£475
❑ UK Quarterly	£295	£175

Overseas subscriptions please add the following postage to the above prices:

	Monthly	Quarterly
Europe	£75	£25
US and Rest of World	£120	£45

- copies will be sent airmail
- please enclose payment with order
- cheques to be in £ sterling
- for details of bulk discounts please call 0171 278 7769
- prices are for orders placed during 1995 only

Indispensable Information for Active Investors

Each month Company REFS brings you a complete statistical service on all UK registered companies with quoted equity shares (this includes fully listed and USMs but excludes investment trusts). The monthly service includes:

Company REFS *Tables Section* - highlighting stock leaders and laggards
Company REFS *Companies Section* - investment statistics for individual companies
All new subscribers receive a complimentary copy of the manual How to Use Company REFS (by Jim Slater).

Name ______ Position ______
Company ______
Type of Business ______
Address ______

Postcode ______ Telephone ______

If I subscribe and am not satisfied with Company REFS I will return it in good condition within 10 days and claim a **FULL CASH REFUND**

☐ **Cheque enclosed** ☐ **Access/Mastercard**
☐ **American express** ☐ **Visa/Barclaycard**
☐ **Diners** ☐ **Invoice my company**

Our purchase order no/ref is: ______

Card no. ______ Expiry Date ______

Order Date ______ **Signature** ______

If paying by credit card or cheque please enclose this order in an envelope and send to:
Hemmington Scott Publishing Limited, City Innovation Centre, 26 - 31 Whiskin Street, London, EC1R 0BP, UK
Registered Office 124-130 Seymour Place, London, W1H 6AA, Registered in England No 1865806 **CRF 941C2**

BUSINESS REPLY SERVICE
Licence No. KE 7015

1

HEMMINGTON SCOTT PUBLISHING LIMITED
CITY INNOVATION CENTRE
26-31 WHISKIN STREET
LONDON
EC1B 1HS

BUSINESS REPLY SERVICE
Licence No. KE 7015

1

HEMMINGTON SCOTT PUBLISHING LIMITED
CITY INNOVATION CENTRE
26-31 WHISKIN STREET
LONDON
EC1B 1HS

PRICE-TO-RESEARCH AND DEVELOPMENT RATIO (PRR)

The PRR is only a useful measure for companies which engage, as a way of life, in a substantial amount of research and development expenditure every year. Companies in pharmaceuticals, electronics, bio-tech and computer software are typical examples. The PRR will, therefore, only be shown in company entries where there has been research and development expenditure of over 1% of market capitalisation as shown by the latest Annual Report.

The PRR is obtained by dividing the market capitalisation of a company by the total research and development expenditure. This is the same as dividing the share price by the research and development expenditure per share. For example, if the market capitalisation of a company is £200m and the research and development expenditure is £5m, the PRR is 40.

The PRR provides a quick and easy check on the relative amounts being spent on research and development by different companies in the same sector. It is also helpful as an investment measure if a company is making losses and in a valuation 'black hole'. On occasions, the PRR can provide startling evidence that such a significant amount is being spent on research and development that the shares *ought to be* a bargain, if and when the company recovers.

Examples include Kewill Systems, which had a very attractive PRR of 2 in January 1993, when the shares were 47p (end of 1993 -265p); Avesco had a PRR of 3 in January 1993, when the shares were only 15p (end of 1993 - 130p after a 1 for 3 rights issue at 63p); Kalamazoo had a PRR of 4 in early 1993, when the shares were 30p (end of 1993 - 100p).

PRR

When the shares of a technology company are in a market black hole because it is still loss-making, the PSR is a more powerful single measure than the PRR. However, one indicator cross-checks the other. For example, a technology company that seems a little expensive on a PSR basis, could still be a buy if its PRR was exceptionally attractive. Conversely, a company with a very attractive PSR might not be spending enough on research, which should give cause for concern.

Companies with attractive PRRs are shown in the tables headed 'Lowest Price-to-R & D Expenditure Ratios'. These give a clear idea of the relative amounts being spent on research and development by companies with major research departments, together with other relevant statistics.

An important caveat is that the allocation of expenditure to research and development can be somewhat arbitrary; different companies may classify the same expenditure in different ways. The figures are unlikely to be materially distorted, however, and, provided the accounting basis is consistent, they can still reveal meaningful trends.

PBV

PRICE-TO-BOOK VALUE (PBV)

The PBV is obtained by dividing the share price of a company by its net asset value per share. The same result is, of course, obtained by dividing the company's market capitalisation by its net assets.

The difficulty with PBV as a meaningful investment criterion is defining the word 'value'. Copyrights, patents and brand names, for example, can be worth little or nothing, or many times their cost or book value. No fair value can really be established unless a competitive auction tests the market. Any valuation made by the board is essentially arbitrary and subjective.

A further problem is that companies treat intangible assets in different ways. Some revalue them in their balance sheets, others write them off completely or in part, immediately or over a period. Comparisons are therefore difficult to make and stark figures can be misleading. **PBV**

Other more tangible assets such as plant and machinery, factories, office buildings, hotels and the like, can also have dubious value. For example, specialised machines that may soon become obsolescent, and factories in the middle of nowhere, are impossible to value accurately. Valuations of assets like these tend to be subjective and book values are often far removed from the underlying true worth.

Benjamin Graham, the dean of value investing, makes the general point that it is unwise to buy a share at a price above its book value. Conscious of the difficulty of valuing most fixed assets, he preferred to buy at two-thirds of current net asset value, taking no account of assets like factories and machinery and after deducting all debt. However, in his time, Graham was spoilt for choice and few such extreme bargains exist today.

In general terms, PBV is a primitive investment measure that can at times provide a small degree of comfort to shareholders in a company. If the book value is well in excess of the share price (a low PBV) it can also point to the possibility of a takeover; however, quality of the assets is all-important.

PRICE-TO-TANGIBLE BOOK VALUE (PTBV)

PTBV

The PTBV is obtained by dividing the share price of a company by its net asset value per share after deducting intangibles. The same result is, of course, obtained by dividing the company's market capitalisation by its tangible net assets.

PTBV

Because of the arbitrary nature of assets like copyrights, patents and goodwill, *Company REFS* provides this harsher measure of a company's net asset value. Excluding all intangibles has the additional advantage of being *consistent,* so that inter-company comparisons can be made on a more even footing. For this reason, the tables of companies with apparently attractive book values have been confined to tangible asset comparisons. The resultant figures should be treated with caution because, in some cases, the intangible assets (that have been deducted) will have a tremendous value, whereas in others they may be worth very little. Also, even the tangible assets may be of questionable value.

GEAR

NET GEARING (GEAR)

A strong cash position is an obvious advantage for a company; conversely, excessive gearing can be dangerous and at times threaten a company's survival.

As a guideline net gearing of over 50% calls for further investigation. This is especially the case if a large proportion of overall borrowings are short-term. A highly-geared company is more vulnerable to changes in interest rates. It is also more vulnerable to a sudden recession or unexpected major strike, as it is more likely to be fully invested and committed operationally.

If the net gearing percentage is worrying, the sector moon should be checked and the sector tables to ascertain the norm for the industry.

The net gearing figure in the key statistics is calculated by taking the total gearing less cash, treasury bills and certificates of deposit and expressing the resultant figure as a percentage of shareholders funds including intangibles, such as brand names, copyrights and goodwill. Note that the cash figure does not include marketable securities as they may be difficult to realise in an emergency. A minus sign indicates negative net gearing and denotes a net cash position (also expressed as a percentage of shareholders' funds including intangibles).

A much fuller explanation of the method of calculation and the implications of gearing is set out in Chapter 5 under GEARING, COVER.

MARGIN

Margin is the ratio of operating profit to turnover. For example, a company with operating profits (trading profit before tax, interest and associates' contribution) of £10m and a turnover of £100m has an operating margin of 10%. Generally speaking, a high margin is a good sign.

For the purpose of calculating margins, *Company REFS* defines operating profits as trading profits before tax, interest, other investment income and any share of associated company profits. Capital profits and losses, and other exceptional items, are also eliminated.

A company's operating margin is a vitally important investment statistic that links price-to-sales ratios and price-earnings ratios. Increasing sales are of much less value if margins are falling drastically. If margins are being maintained or are expanding, they quickly translate into increased net profits.

The figure in the shaded, key statistics panel gives the operating margin based on the last full year's accounts. Other information regarding the margin's trend and its average over five years can be found in the 'Historical Performance' panel.

There are a number of caveats to bear in mind when considering margins as an investment measure:-

Margin

1. Very high margins invite competition. Unless the barriers to entry are very strong, other companies will be attracted to the industry. Ideally a company will combine high margins with products or services that are 'unique' and difficult to emulate; well-patented products are a good example.

2. Very low margins obviously add to the risk of any investment. A small fall in sales can have a disproportionate and sometimes disastrous effect on profits. Equally, the slightest upward movement can have a very beneficial effect.

3. Companies with a history of low margins, in industries that have become used to them, find it very difficult to increase their margins. Treat with scepticism extravagant claims about future increases in margin.

4. The significant improvement of margins is usually based upon some kind of product or service enhancement. Try to identify these from press cuttings or brokers' circulars. Whenever possible, ask management for a detailed explanation of their policy and their long-term goals for margins.

5. Major changes in margins frequently occur as a result of new top management. The recent record of margins should therefore be looked at in this context.

   Seek an explanation if a company has had the same management for years and margins appear to be changing substantially. A downward movement could be due, for example, to a price war; an improvement the result of new and improved products.

6. Very choppy margin records usually indicate businesses in industries that are subject to periodic price wars and/or are very cyclical. Beware therefore of buying into such a company during

a period of very high margins, unless there is very strong evidence that it will be different this time around.

Margin

The columns of moons show the margin relative to the market and the company's sector. A full black moon shows relatively high margins, a half-filled moon average ones and a blank moon relatively low margins.

ROCE

RETURN ON CAPITAL EMPLOYED (ROCE)

The ROCE is calculated by expressing the operating profit before tax as a percentage of the year-end capital employed.

The main features of ROCE as an investment measure are as follows:-

1. High ROCE (in the region of 20% or more) is a validation of a company's competitive advantage. It indicates that the company has something special to offer - products or services that command a high return. It usually follows that margins are above average. The trend of both capital employed and margins is, therefore, of considerable importance.

2. Comparison of the ROCE of a company with other companies in its sector is a far more pertinent measure than comparison with the market as a whole. Companies with low returns are always suspect because they are in danger of becoming loss-making if trading conditions deteriorate. Companies with exceptionally high returns may invite competition for their products or services, unless they are fully protected by patents or in some other way.

3. The ROCE of a company should always be compared with the current cost of borrowing. If the ROCE is significantly higher, further borrowing adds to EPS; if the ROCE is lower, further borrowing will reduce EPS.

ROCE

4. Companies with low ROCE are often the subject of changes in management control which, in turn, are frequently followed by a rights issue. The most acid test of new management is whether or not it is able to lift the return on capital employed.

5. The obvious attraction of a high ROCE is that a more than average amount of profits can be ploughed back into the business for the advantage of shareholders. The plough-back is then employed again at the higher than average rate and helps to generate further growth in EPS. For this reason, a high ROCE is usually a common denominator of great growth stocks.

ROCE has not been calculated for banks and insurance companies. The ROCE of most property companies and of some financial companies should be viewed with caution, as the statistic may not be particularly meaningful.

Capital employed is the sum of ordinary and preference share capital plus reserves, debentures, loan stocks, all borrowings including obligations under finance leases, bank overdraft, minority interests and provisions. Deductions include investments in associated companies. The basic idea is to arrive at a final figure that will tell you how much money (whatever the source) is being employed in the operation of a business. The resultant figure is then compared with the operating profits before tax, exceptional items, interest, dividends payable and share of profits or losses of investments in associated companies. The percentage this figure bears to adjusted capital employed gives an investor a measure of the kind of return the business can produce on the capital employed within it.

A significant problem arises with goodwill, brand names, patents, copyrights, newspaper titles and the like. There is no doubt that intangible assets can be immensely valuable, but the accounting treatment of them can vary considerably. For example, brand names

ROCE

sometimes have no value in the balance sheet and, at others, they are written up in value to a significant proportion of the net assets. The difficulty is that no fair value can really be established unless a competitive auction tests the market. Any valuation made by the board is essentially arbitrary and, by definition, subjective.

In *Company REFS* all intangibles are excluded. This treatment has the following advantages:-

1. It is consistent.

2. It measures the operating efficiency of a business by comparing operating profits with operating assets.

3. It does not change the operating efficiency of a business being acquired. For example, an acquiring company may pay double tangible asset value for a business. If the resultant goodwill were left in the balance sheet, this would halve the ROCE of the business in the accounts of the acquiring company. In fact, the operating efficiency of the business acquired would remain unchanged and this is reflected in the *Company REFS* figures which exclude goodwill.

The *Company REFS* approach of excluding intangibles is flattering to very acquisitive companies that might be over-paying for the businesses they acquire. The writing-off of the goodwill paid for businesses acquired will result in higher returns on capital employed in the accounts of acquiring companies. The high returns are being made by the operating assets, not on the purchase consideration (including goodwill) paid by the acquiring companies. *Company REFS* readers should bear this in mind when judging the ROCE of conglomerates and other particularly acquisitive companies.

INDEX

INDEX AND MARKET OVERALL

Each share is included in one of the following four categories and ranked according to its position. The table below summarises the distribution in September 1994:-

	Including Investment Trusts	**Excluding Investment Trusts**
FT-SE 100	100	99
FT-SE Mid 250	250	215
FT-SE SmallCap	516	428
FT-SE Actuaries All-Share	866	742
Non-Index	1028	857
Total	**1894**	**1599**

The position of a share in its index at the end of each month is determined by its market capitalisation. This should always be compared with the position of the company in the market overall to give an immediate idea of whether or not a share is a contender for promotion to or demotion from an index. Its market ranking is given immediately beneath its index position. Although investment trusts are not included in the Companies Volume of *Company REFS*, they are taken into account for index ranking.

In practice, shares that are likely to be promoted or demoted by the Review Panel at its quarterly meeting are usually at the extremities of their index. For example, a contender for promotion to the FT-SE 100 Index might be number one in the Mid 250 Index and could be as high as 90th in the market overall.

Conversely, a contender for demotion from the Mid 250 Index to the SmallCap Index might be 249 in the Mid 250 Index and 370 in the market overall. As there are 100 shares in the FT-SE 100 and 250 in the Mid 250 Index, this would mean, all other things being equal, that the company in question should really be number 20 in the SmallCap Index.

The importance of promotion to and demotion from one index to another, or in or out of the indices altogether, should not be underestimated. Many institutions only buy shares in the main indices and most tracker funds are compelled to buy a promoted share and sell a demoted one. Advance warning of the likelihood of promotion or demotion is therefore crucially important.

The Tables Volume shows the 15 top candidates for promotion and demotion in each of the indices and the 15 candidates for promotion from outside the indices.

THE MOONS

Moons

Although I have referred to the two columns of moons several times when examining the various investment measures, they are well worth a special mention in their own right.

Any statistic is of little value unless it is examined in relation to other statistics of a similar nature. Clearly, the most relevant ones are the market as a whole (first column - M) and the average of other companies in the sector (second column - S).

The moons should be used as gauges, to show at a glance if company ratios or percentages are relatively high (a full black moon is the highest), median (a half moon) or relatively low (a clear moon is the lowest) for each key investment criterion. The moons are calibrated to show the position of a company in the market as a whole and in its sector. For example, in a sector containing seven companies, if the company under review was in 4th position, the sector moon would be half full.

Moons

It is of obvious interest to compare the return on capital employed and the margins of a company with other companies in its sector. If a company enjoys a higher-than-average return on capital and better margins than others in it sector, it is usually a strong sign that the company enjoys a competitive advantage.

It is also interesting to know how much sales and research expenditure you can buy per share and compare the figures with competitors in the same sector.

Even the more traditional investment measures such as price-earnings ratios, dividend yields and price-to-book values often reveal interesting anomalies when compared with the market as a whole and a company's peer group. For example, a share may have an attractively low PER against the market, but a high one for its sector. This may be because the growth prospects are better than the sector average, in which case this should be reflected in a lower-than-average PEG factor.

The moons provide analysts with a valuable tool that quickly points to anomalies worth further investigation by turning to the detailed sector statistics and/or the rest of the company entry.

KEY DATES

Key Dates

Underneath the shaded panel of key statistics you will find KEY DATES in a small panel like this one:

KEY DATES	
next AR year end	31-Mar-95
int xd (3.90p)	9-Nov-92
fin xd (9.60p)	14-Jun-93
int results	3-Nov-93
int xd (4.30p)	8-Nov-93
year end	31-Mar-94
prelim results	31-May-94
annual report	14-Jun-94
fin xd (11.2p)	14-Jun-94
agm	8-Jul-94

Key Dates

Key dates are particularly important for fast-growing smaller companies, which usually have their moment in the sun around the time of their preliminary and interim results. The AGM date is also of vital importance as the chairman frequently uses the meeting to make a statement about future prospects.

A company growing at say 30% per annum on an historic multiple of 20 (a PEG of 0.66) would attract immediate investment interest when it announced another year of 30% growth, coupled with an optimistic forecast. The historic multiple would then cease to be of real interest and attention would focus on the prospective multiple for the year ahead. If the consensus forecast was for another 30% growth in earnings, the prospective multiple would fall to about 13 (provided the share price remained constant). For a company growing at 30% per annum, this would be an obvious bargain and the shares would almost certainly rise sharply.

Of course, the shares were cheap a month before the results. However, the announcement turned fancy into fact and the all-important focus of interest switched immediately to the following year.

This principle applies to all companies, but is exaggerated with fast-growing smaller companies, because most of the research material and press comment on them is relatively sparse other than when they are announcing their results and having their moment in the sun.

The ex-dividend dates are of particular interest to income funds and income-conscious investors.

2

SECTOR AND ACTIVITIES ANALYSIS

To the immediate left of the shaded panel of key statistics, two panels describe the company's sector and analyse its activities, by product and geographically:

SECTOR

Health care.

ACTIVITIES ANALYSIS (94AR)		T/O	Pr
Clinical laboratories	%	44	59
Healthcare services	%	35	17
Environmental services	%	13	12
Medical equipment	%	5	12
Other activities	%	3	–5
Europe	%	41	72
North America	%	46	20
Asia/Pacific	%	13	8

Sector

SECTOR

Only brief sector details are given in the company entry. More detailed information can be found in the analysis of the sector in the Tables Volume. This includes a list of all its constituent companies together with composite statistics. Tables of comparative figures enable important statistics like ROCE, MARGIN, PERs, PEGs and PSRs to be compared. The subject of sectors is fully covered in chapter seven.

ACTIVITIES ANALYSIS

Activities Analysis

Analysing a company's business by product or activity provides a useful check on its exposure to market forces in the various industries in which it operates. For example, a diversified business may be in building supplies, engineering and distribution of consumer products. The weighting of turnover and profit in each sector provides a fix on the company's exposure to the trade cycle and to trends and developments in those industries.

It is also pertinent to note any activity that has a large turnover but relatively small profit (or even a loss). This can sometimes highlight the need for a reorganisation or the possibility of a takeover. Conversely, any activity with a very high profit in relation to its turnover could be vulnerable to increased competition, unless there are strong barriers to entry.

Geographical spread provides an indication of the degree of a company's involvement in an acknowledged growth area and its exposure to currency risks and adverse developments such as the recent Malaysian ban on trade with British firms. Geographical analysis is always by destination (when available). Of particular interest, in early 1994, is the exposure to Europe, which may or may not be on the brink of recovery, and the Far East, which is one of the fastest-expanding regions in the world.

Activities Analysis

The analysis of both turnover and profits is extracted from the latest annual report. The bracketed information indicates the source - (93AR), for example, represents the 1993 annual report.

Percentages in the profits column are calculated before central overheads and central income. Discontinued businesses are usually excluded from both columns.

When there is an overall net profit, the plus percentages add up to +100% (rounded off, so sometimes 99% or 101%) and any losses are expressed as a percentage of total profits. If there is an overall net loss, the minus percentages add up to -100% and any profits are expressed as a percentage of total losses.

Example 1

	£m	%	
Industrial Plastics	25	8	100
Plastics Packaging	30	10	
Agricultural Products	256	82	
Heat Exchangers	(125)	-40	
Net operating profit	186		

Profits on agricultural products are 82% of the total profits of £311m. As there is an overall net profit, losses on heat exchangers of £125m are expressed as a percentage (in this case 40%) of £311m.

Activities Analysis

Example 2

	£m	%	
Industrial Plastics	(25)	- 8	
Plastics Packaging	(30)	-10	-100
Agricultural Products	(256)	-82	
Heat Exchangers	125	40	
Net operating loss	(186)		

Losses on agricultural products are 82% of the total losses of £311m. As there is an overall net loss, profits of £125m on heat exchangers are expressed as a percentage (in this case 40%) of £311m.

Example 3

	£m	%
Agricultural Products	(256)	-100
Industrial Plastics	25	10
Plastics Packaging	30	12
Heat Exchangers	125	49
Net operating loss	(76)	

Losses on agricultural products are 100% of the total losses of £256m. As there is an overall net loss, profits on other activities are expressed as a percentage of £256m.

Further examples and a more detailed explanation are given in the Technical Appendix.

Activities Analysis

Companies have wide discretion in the way they can present an analysis of their activities, so the figures should be viewed simply as a broad-brush indicator. The analyses are not directly comparable between different companies, even in the same sector, as they may have been prepared on different bases.

3

EARNINGS, DIVIDEND ESTIMATES AND HISTORICAL PERFORMANCE

Below ACTIVITIES ANALYSIS are two panels mainly devoted to the company's earnings and dividend. They display a range of historic and forecast statistical information, including five-year averages and trends. Similar information is given for sales, margin and ROCE.

Before considering these in detail, it is essential to understand how *Company REFS* has approached this complicated subject.

EARNINGS PER SHARE (EPS)

EPS

Since the introduction of FRS3, the Accounting Standards Board's newest regulation regarding earnings per share, calculating and using EPS data has become a minefield. Three different measures of EPS have become accepted and attention has been focused on what should be included and excluded from the final figure.

EPS

Although FRS3 has complicated the issue, investors should regard its introduction as a good thing. The development of two new earnings measures, IIMR headline earnings and normalised earnings, has exposed the sloppiness of much of the work that previously passed as investment analysis. For the first time, EPS, PERs and PEGs can be compared and are now meaningful statistics.

FRS3 now governs the presentation of profit and loss accounts. It has become mandatory for all UK companies reporting financial accounting periods ending after 22nd June 1993.

Prior to FRS3, exceptional items had to be deducted from trading profits but extraordinary items could be shown below the line, where they did not affect earnings per share. Exceptional items were those that were thought to be unusual but germane to the business and therefore likely to recur in some form in future years: they included unusually large bad debts and major strikes, both of which are part of the cost of being in business. Extraordinary items, like discontinuing a business, were excluded because they were thought unlikely to recur.

The predominance of the PER as an investment measure resulted in many directors striving to maintain a high level of EPS. Too much latitude was given to finance directors (and boards) to decide whether an event was exceptional or extraordinary. This often resulted in unusual profits being classified as exceptional and unusual losses as extraordinary.

With FRS3, the ASB has now lumped all exceptional and extraordinary items together and makes no distinction between the two - now they all have to be deducted from (or added to) profits and, as a result, from (or to) earnings per share. This has the desirable effect of removing the decision-making process (whether an item is extraordinary or exceptional) from management, but the undesirable effect of distorting the results of all companies, including many with items of expenditure or revenue which should *genuinely* be classified as extraordinary.

EPS

The ASB does not object to companies showing their own version of earnings per share in parallel with the mandatory FRS3 presentation. It does, however, insist that the management's interpretation is reconciled with FRS3 earnings per share, and presented on a consistent basis over time.

IIMR Headline Earnings

IIMR EPS

In the minds of many observers, the new rules have gone a step too far. FRS3 is now seen as a kind of dustbin, a catch-all that makes historic earnings per share a meaningless statistic. As a result, the Institute of Investment Management and Research (IIMR) has recommended analysts to make adjustments to the profits resulting from the strict application of FRS3. The intention is to arrive at a realistic assessment of the trading profit made during the year. The main distinction between FRS3 and so-called IIMR headline earnings is that non-trading and capital items are included in the former and excluded from the latter.

In the Appendix, you will find a table showing full details of inclusions and exclusions. Some important examples of inclusions in IIMR headline earnings are all trading profits and losses (even if abnormal in size), costs of fundamental reorganisation of the business, and profits and losses arising from the trading activities of businesses discontinued during the year or businesses acquired during the year. Examples of exclusions are profits and losses on the sale of fixed assets or businesses, items relating to prior periods, the effect of any change in accounting policy and the correction of previous accounting errors. The intention is to arrive at the *trading profit* made during the accounting period.

At one time, it looked as if IIMR headline earnings would become the recognised standard for broker and press reporting. However, the jury is still out on what is essentially a compromise between the old and new reporting standards. The back pages of the *Financial Times* have adopted

IIMR EPS

the IIMR headline EPS for quotation purposes, but brokers' circulars and press comment are tending to quote FRS3 EPS and also what have become known as normalised EPS figures, which exclude all exceptional items.

Norm EPS

Normalised Earnings

Differences between IIMR headline earnings and normalised earnings include such items as very large redundancy costs, fundamental reorganisation costs and exceptional tax charges. There is a subjective element in deciding exactly what to exclude from normalised earnings. The criteria used by *Company REFS* are the following:-

1. The amount must be sufficiently large to have a material and distorting effect on the earnings per share trend.

2. It must be clearly identifiable and separate from normal trading.

3. It must be unusual in nature and not expected to recur in the normal course of events.

4. It will have been or is likely to be ignored by most analysts in establishing an actual earnings performance base, upon which to build future estimates.

All of these four criteria must be satisfied for any adjustment to be made to IIMR headline earnings. If any adjustments are made, the tax effect is also calculated and brought into the resultant 'normalised' earnings figure.

Normalised earnings possess three important characteristics:-

1. They reflect the underlying *trading* performance of the company.

2. They can be used as a *measure* of performance against expectations.

3. They clarify the *historic record of the operating performance* of a company.

Norm EPS

The main limitation of normalised earnings is that they reflect the results achieved by the business during an accounting period when a company had a certain structure which may have changed. For example, normalised earnings include the results of trading businesses which have been discontinued or sold and only part of the results of companies acquired during the year.

You can see that, in a way, the whole exercise of calculating EPS has gone full circle. FRS3 became necessary because there was so much abuse, but it was so draconian that analysts have found it necessary to calculate their way back to a kind of pre-FRS3 position. The main difference today is that the basis of the calculations does not now depend on the judgement of a company's directors, and every exceptional item is analysed in a harsher light.

Maintainable Earnings

Maintainable EPS

When it comes to forecasting earnings per share, there is one further complication - to estimate future EPS, analysts find it necessary to establish a base of 'maintainable' earnings. These are calculated by taking out any non-forecastable exceptionals from normalised earnings and adjusting them (including notional interest adjustments) to eliminate discontinued businesses and bring in a full year's profits (or losses) for businesses acquired during the year. The result is that maintainable earnings reflect the likely results of a business given its structure at the time of making the calculation.

Maintainable earnings are used by brokers in establishing a base from which to project estimates of future EPS. The figures shown in brokers' one and two year estimates are in almost all cases based on these kinds of assumptions.

Maintainable EPS

You can see from the foregoing that the calculations for growth in EPS usually take normalised EPS as a base figure. The following year's earnings will be estimated by brokers based on the business as presently constituted. The resultant growth rate calculations do not then necessarily represent growth in the underlying business, unless there has been no change in its constitution.

A large number of brokers making forecasts and a small standard deviation will give some reassurance that the consensus estimate is reliable and well-based. In contrast, only two brokers making estimates with a wide variation between them mean that the consensus figure should be treated as highly suspect.

Professional investors will be interested to study the Appendix in more detail. This gives chapter and verse on the calculation of IIMR headline earnings and the *Company REFS* policy for normalised earnings. Active private investors can work on the basis that *Company REFS* has calculated normalised earnings in a meaningful way. Taken in conjunction with the brokers' consensus estimates, the *Company REFS* normalised earnings figures should give investors a good idea of the accepted view of each company's EPS and its growth rate.

Earnings, Dividend Estimates

EARNINGS, DIVIDEND ESTIMATES

Usually, three years of EPS are shown, as in the panel shown below:

EARNINGS, DIVIDEND ESTIMATES				
		94AR	95E	96E
norm eps	p	47.6	54.4	64.6
change	p		–	+0.40
brokers	n		16	16
std dev	p		2.05	5.29
growth	%	52.0	14.3	18.8
per	x	20.7	18.1	15.2
dps	p	15.5	17.9	20.7
div yield	%	1.97	2.28	2.63

Earnings, Dividend Estimates

The first column shows historic normalised EPS and is marked 'AR' if the figures are based on the last annual report or 'PA' as soon as the following year's preliminary announcement has been made. The second and third columns show the brokers' consensus estimate (if any) for the next two years. When estimates are available, the letter 'E' appears after the year in question.

On the next line, the word 'change' indicates the amount by which the EPS consensus estimate has increased or decreased within the past month. If material, this can have a significant effect on the share price as a change in the trend of news-flow can be the cause of substantial buying or selling of a company's shares.

The next line simply indicates the number of brokers who have made estimates of EPS for the years in question. In most cases, brokers make estimates for both years, but sometimes they only forecast one year ahead.

Obviously, the more brokers forecasting, the more reliable the consensus estimate. This is especially so if there is a low standard deviation between estimates. If, for example, the standard deviation is 0.50p on consensus estimated EPS of 7.00p, two-thirds of the brokers' estimates can be expected to fall within plus or minus 0.50p of the consensus estimate of 7.0p.

If the estimates are wildly different, the resultant consensus can be unreliable. If they are all at or around the same broad level, they can still be wrong, but at least they provide a stronger degree of comfort.

The growth rate percentage on the next line is a highly significant figure; it is the biggest single factor to consider when deciding if the PER is high, low or about right. However, growth rates are only reliable if growth is reasonably steady with only the occasional hiccup.

Earnings, Dividend Estimates

Any company that is recovering from a major setback is not growing in the true sense of the word.

The easiest way of seeing quickly if a company is a true growth share is to look at the graph and, in particular, the trend of EPS. The trend of past results and future forecasts needs to be strongly in an upward direction. The minimum REFS requirement for a growth share is at least four years of consecutive EPS growth, either in the last four years, if there is no forecast, or a combination of past growth (usually two years) and forecast growth (usually the current year and the one ahead).

If a company passes this test, then the growth rate percentage can be used to calculate the PEG as follows:-

$$\frac{\textit{Year ahead PER}}{\textit{Growth rate for year ahead}} = \textit{prospective PEG}$$

A PEG of one or under is usually very attractive. Clearly it is less attractive if the brokers' consensus estimate and rate of growth tails off in the following year. The PEG factor is shown in the shaded panel of key statistics.

The PER is clearly indicated and calculated in each of the three years based on the normalised EPS figures whenever available. As I have already explained, the PER of a company is a one-dimensional measure and has to be looked at in relation to the growth record and prospects and other investment factors such as gearing.

DPS stands for 'dividends per share' and a consensus estimate is given for future years whenever estimates are available from brokers. The prospective dividend yield is also calculated in each year based on the consensus estimate when available.

HISTORICAL PERFORMANCE

Historical Performance

The distinction between normalised, IIMR and FRS3 EPS has already been explained in detail. For analysis purposes, normalised EPS gives the best indication of the underlying trend, but IIMR and FRS3 statistics are also given for comparison. When FRS3 and normalised earnings are exactly the same, or very similar, it is usually a sign of a clean and easy-to-understand set of accounts - a small clearing in the accounting jungle.

HISTORICAL PERFORMANCE					
		94AR	5Y-av	Y↓	Tr%
norm eps	p	47.6	30.3	1↓	+11.3
IIMR eps	p	47.6	34.0[3]		+42.9
FRS3 eps	p	48.0	33.6[3]		+42.0
cflow ps	p	65.6	56.2[4]	1↓	+9.18
tax rate	%	34.8	32.7	2↓	+3.02
dps	p	15.5	12.9		+6.62
sales ps	£	9.84	9.12	1↓	+9.23
margin	%	13.6	10.6	2↓	-3.92
ROCE	%	21.9	16.7	2↓	+0.64

In the panel above, the 5-year average (5Y-av) column is self-explanatory. The Y column indicates the number of years in which EPS, for example, has declined in the previous five. The trend of normalised EPS is a key figure indicating the annual growth rate. However, any company with more than one down year is unlikely to be a growth share, unless there has been a recent major change in its management and/or prospects.

Cash flow per share is a useful cross-check against normalised EPS to ascertain whether or not creative acounting has been at work, to check if the dividend is safe and to project future levels of liquidity and gearing. Further implications are analysed in the explanation of PCF in the table of key statistics.

All the trend figures under Tr% show the trend of annual growth (+) or annual decline (-) and are based on a minimum of three years' figures.

Historical Performance

The tax rate shows the average rate of taxation which the company has provided against its reported pre-tax profit on an FRS3 basis. The overall rate takes into account corporation tax, deferred tax, overseas taxation, double-tax relief and any unrelieved ACT write-offs. Prior year adjustments are also included (as they tend to recur), but the taxation on any share of associated company results is ignored.

DPS stands for dividends per share. Dividends are a vitally important investment measure. High-yielding shares tend to beat the market and a cut in dividend is regarded as a major setback for any company. A firmly rising trend of dividend payments in line with a trend of increasing earnings, and well covered by cash flow, is the ideal scenario. It follows that dividends per share and the trend should therefore be cross-checked with the normalised EPS and cash flow figures. The forecast dividend per share in the panel of estimates above should also be checked to make sure that the increasing trend of dividends looks as if it is likely to continue.

The sales per share figure and the trend of sales are of particular interest when considering margins. The ideal scenario is steadily increasing sales coupled with the gradually increasing margins that would normally be expected with the benefit of larger scale.

The PSR in the panel of key statistics and the sector comparison are useful cross-checks on whether or not a company's sales are unusually high or low in relation to its share price and its industry. Margins should also be checked with the panel of key statistics to note the sector comparison. The trend of margins is also crucially important - expanding sales at the expense of margins can easily lead to profitless prosperity.

For further information on the importance and significance of margins, see the more detailed exposition of margins in the guide to the panel of key statistics.

Historical Performance

The ROCE (return on capital employed) is one of the most important single investment statistics. A high ROCE validates a company's competitive advantage and is usually accompanied by higher than average margins for the sector.

The trend of return on capital employed is of considerable importance and also the sector comparison, which can be evaluated from the panel of key statistics and the composite sector statistics. In particular, companies with exceptionally high returns may invite competition for their products or services and a falling return on capital employed can indicate that this problem is beginning to bite.

In the 5-year average column, you will occasionally see a small number just to the right of each statistic. This superscript appears when five years of statistics are not available; in that event, the small number indicates the number of years on which the average and the trend are based.

4

THE GRAPH, ACTIVITIES AND OUTLOOK

The top left hand side of the entry, which includes the graph, a description of the company's activities and an outline of its prospects, will look familiar to many investors. We believe, however, that the combination of historic and forecast earnings per share with actual and relative share price charts provides an exceptional amount of information for potential and existing shareholders. Here is a typical entry:

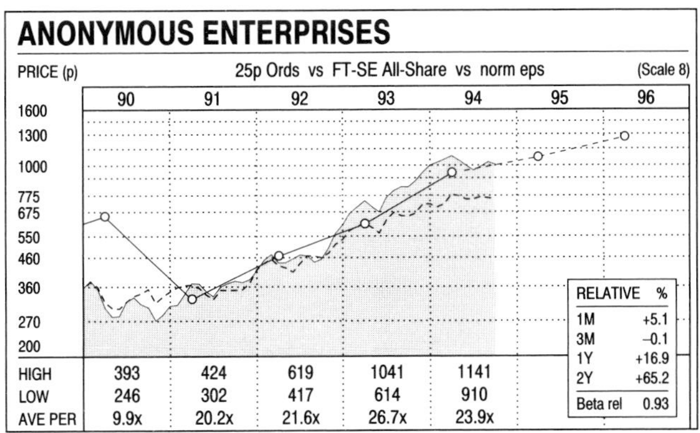

SHARE PRICE GRAPH

Share Price Graph

The share price graph presents in graphic form the following information:-

1. Year-by-year EPS, adjusted to a normalised basis when historic (a solid line joining the very small circles on the financial year-end dates) and based on brokers' forecasts for the future (a broken line between the very small circles).

2. The average monthly share price shown by the solid line forming the boundary of the shaded area, which therefore highlights the share price movement.

3. The relative strength of the shares against the market, as measured by the FT-SE Actuaries All-Share Index, shown by the dotted line. The angle of inclination of the relative strength trend line shows if the company's share price has been moving up or down in relation to the market. The company's share price may have been increasing or decreasing, but the relative strength trend line tells you if the share price has performed better or worse than the market as a whole.

4. The highs and lows of the share price (adjusted as with all other statistics for rights and scrip issues etc) over the last five years.

5. The average PER each year, based on month-end PERs calculated on the latest annual normalised EPS.

6. The relative strength (plus or minus) of the shares against the All-Share Index over the last month, three months, one year and two years. The dotted line shows the relative strength over the whole period covered by the graph.

Share Price Graph

7. The Beta factor which indicates how rapidly and consistently a company's shares move up and down with the market. The market's Beta coefficient is one; shares with a Beta larger than one are more volatile than the market and shares with a Beta of under one are less risky.

A logarithmic scale has been employed for two reasons. Firstly, it measures vertical movement on a proportional basis; this ensures that a given percentage movement will always be represented by the same distance on the vertical scale. If, for instance, the share price had doubled from 40p to 80p, the vertical movement would be exactly the same if the price doubled again to 160p.

Secondly, a logarithmic scale enables a direct comparison to be made between the graphs of different companies featured in *Company REFS* irrespective of share prices, provided that their vertical scales are on the same height ratio (the highest price divided by the lowest price on the scale). Logarithmic graphs on the same scale can be overlaid, but this kind of comparison cannot be made with graphs on a linear scale.

The graphs overleaf show how two companies would appear on a linear scale and a logarithmic scale. The assumptions are that the share price of company A was increasing by the same percentage each year, whereas company B's share price was increasing by the same amount of pence per share each year. As you can see, a logarithmic scale gives a far better visual impression of the year-by-year rate of growth and shows clearly if it is slowing down or accelerating.

Share Price Graph

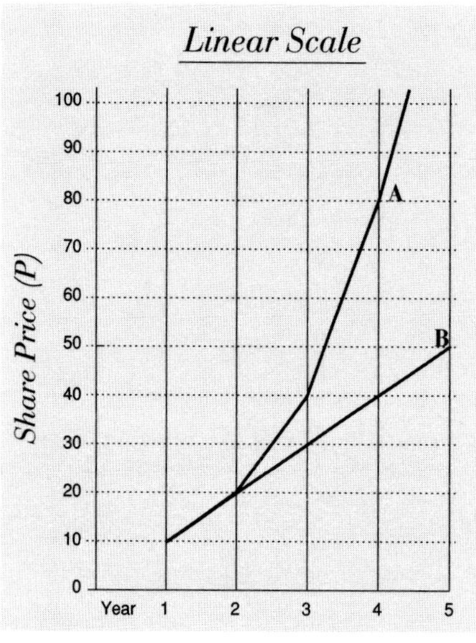

Company A: Share price increasing at the same rate each year produces a hyperbola

Company B: Share price increasing by the same amount each year produces a straight line

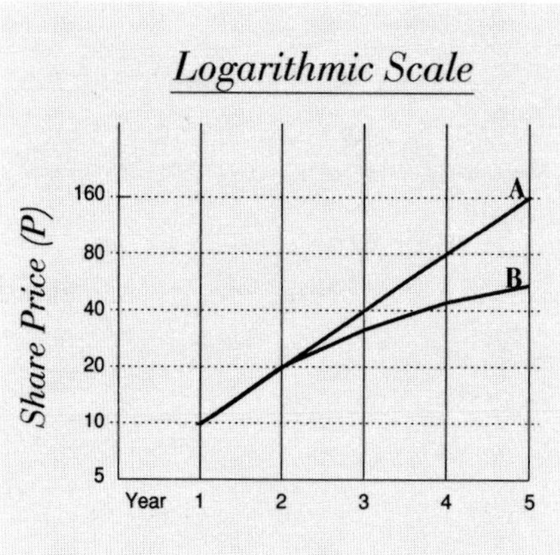

Company A: Share price increasing at the same rate each year produces a straight line

Company B: Share price increasing by the same amount each year produces a shallow curve, showing that the rate of growth is slowing down

The way that EPS have been fitted on the same base as the plot of the share price is described as 're-basing' and is explained in detail in the Technical Appendix. There is no doubt that EPS and the price of a growth share are umbilically linked over the long term. The 20-year graph of BTR illustrates this well.

Share Price Graph

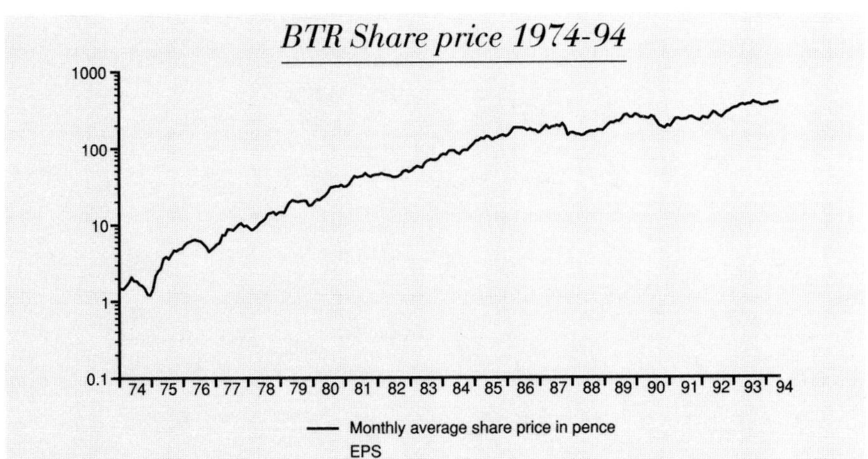

The trend of EPS is therefore of major interest in identifying a growth share. The normal *Company REFS* requirement for a growth share is four years of consecutive EPS growth, either over the last four years, if there is no forecast, or a combination of past growth (usually two years) and future forecast growth (usually the current year and the one ahead). The trend of the EPS line on the graph is of crucial importance as the first visual indication of whether or not a share can be classified as a growth share.

The trend of the average PER is also of vital importance as it indicates if there is scope for a further status change. Usually, as a company becomes increasingly acknowledged as a growth share, its PER rises in step with the company's improving status. If, for example, a PER had risen from say, 7 to 30, there would almost certainly be little remaining scope for a further status change. The PEG in the panel of key statistics will indicate if the share is over-priced or if the growth rate justifies the present price.

The small panel headed RELATIVE % gives details of the relative strength of the share against the FT-SE Actuaries All-Share Index. Of particular interest are the one and three month figures which might give an early warning signal that something is wrong. Great growth shares often pause for breath, but prolonged lack of relative strength can be an indication of something more serious.

Activities and Outlook

ACTIVITIES AND OUTLOOK

The activities of each company are outlined under this heading. Other information includes the company's telephone number, the name and contact number of its registrar and the name of its stockbroker. The activities are also analysed by product or service and geographically under ACTIVITIES ANALYSIS.

ACTIVITIES: Development, manufacture and sale of specialised products and services for the healthcare sector. **TEL:** (0171) 278 7769. **REGISTRAR:** Barkers, Leeds. Tel: (01966) 473926 **BROKERS:** Bullish Securities **OUTLOOK:** (13 Jun-94) AR: ch - "All our subsidiaries are now trading profitably. I am confident that you will share in the even greater success of your company in the year to March 1995".

OUTLOOK gives a flavour of the most recent price-sensitive comment on the future outlook emanating from the Chairman's or Chief Executive's comments in the Annual Report, Interim Report or at the AGM. Any announcements by the company are included if they refer to the company's future prospects.

If there has been an announcement of a change of chief executive within the previous twelve months, this is shown after OUTLOOK under the heading of CEO CHANGE. There is also a list of all CEO changes in the Tables Volume.

In the event of a rights issue, suspension or takeover, details will be given as the last item in the panel.

5

SHARE CAPITAL, HOLDINGS, DEALINGS AND GEARING AND COVER

Below ACTIVITIES AND OUTLOOK two panels break down each company's share capital, list its major shareholders and provide further information on its debt position and interest and dividend cover.

SHARE CAPITAL, HOLDINGS, DEALINGS

Share Capital, Holdings, Dealings

Each class of share is listed showing the number in issue and a description. Preference shares, warrants and convertibles are also included, when applicable:

SHARE CAPITAL, HOLDINGS, DEALINGS			
31.9m 25p Ords (Maj 28.8%, Dirs 2.04% [d]).			
National Pens Tstee Co	%	6.23	
HS Staff Superan'tn Fd	%	3.67	
Monument Group	%	3.15	
Sloane Asset Management	%	15.7	
D I Barlow (ce)	k	175	2+
D S Watt (fd)	k	3.00	
Sir Philip Marlowe CBE * (ch)	k	5.00	
J Rockford	%	1.45	2+
Dr R Kimble OBE	k	6.50	

Share Capital, Holdings, Dealings

The total percentage held by major shareholders and directors is noted after each class of share, unless the holdings are below 0.01%. Directors with large holdings are included under directors, not under major shareholders.

Only major shareholders of the most actively-traded class of share are listed. These are shown in size order and if a major shareholding has increased or decreased within the last nine months this is indicated by a figure (how many months ago) and a plus or minus sign (to show buying or selling).

In the panel, it is only possible to list nine major shareholders including directors. Usually, this will result in a maximum of five directors and four major shareholders.

The size of shareholdings are shown as follows:

1% or more ....% (percentage of shares in issue)
1,000,000 or more ....m (millions of shares)
1,000 or more ....k (thousands of shares)
under 1,000 ....n (number of shares)

Directors' shareholdings in the first class of share will be listed in this order: executive chairman, managing director or chief executive, finance director, non-executive chairman, executive directors (in annual report order) and non-executive directors (also in annual report order). Dealings are indicated with a figure and a plus or minus sign in exactly the same way as for major shareholdings. Non-beneficial directors' holdings under 3% are ignored but family holdings are aggregated with the beneficial holdings (any family dealings are shown seperately in the monthly schedule of detailed directors' dealings). Very large non-beneficial holdings are shown under major shareholdings in the name of the actual beneficial shareholder.

Share Capital, Holdings, Dealings

When any director has dealt during the preceding six months, the notation [d] will appear after the particular class of share. The notation is to alert you to refer to the detailed monthly table of directors' dealings.

An August 1993 study by Smith New Court demonstrated that by following directors' dealings, an investor can out-perform the market. In Chapter 8 there is a further explanation of the significance of directors' dealings and a number of points of fine-tuning.

Gearing, Cover

GEARING, COVER

GEARING, COVER (94AR)			
intangibles		Incl	Excl
net gearing	%	−1.77	−1.89
cash	%	37.6	38.5
gross gearing	%	35.8	36.6
under 5 yrs	%	35.8	36.6
under 1 yr	%	4.18	4.27
quick ratio		r	2.11
current ratio		r	2.56
interest cover		x	22.9
dividend cover		x	3.70

This panel of figures gives an insight into the structure of a company's balance sheet. In particular, the overall level of borrowings (gross gearing), how much is short and long-term, borrowings less cash (net gearing), short-term liquidity and the cash position (if any). Other useful statistics include the extent to which interest payments are covered by profits and dividends by earnings.

The first column of figures, headed Incl., shows the percentage of net gearing, cash, gross gearing and one- and five-year gearing in relation to shareholders' funds (share capital plus reserves, less preference capital redeemable within 12 months). The second column, headed Excl., is a

Gearing, Cover

much harsher measure, as all intangibles, such as brand names, copyrights and goodwill, have been deducted from shareholders' funds.

Net gearing is expressed as the percentage of total borrowings (less cash) to shareholders' funds. A minus figure indicates nil net gearing and denotes a net cash position, which is also expressed as a percentage of shareholders' funds.

The cash percentage figures also include near cash assets such as Treasury bills and certificates of deposit. Marketable securities are not included in near cash. This is a harsh measure which assumes that they may be difficult to realise in an emergency.

The cash percentage is shown gross (i.e. borrowings are not deducted), so do not be misled by a particularly high figure. Many companies can borrow large sums, so the cash percentage should always be viewed against gross gearing.

There are several reasons why investors should be particularly aware of the perils of high gearing:-

1. Any company with high gearing, which includes bank and other short-term borrowings, is likely to be very sensitive to changes in interest rates.

2. A highly-geared company can be very vulnerable, and can fail completely, during a liquidity crisis, especially if most of its borrowings are short-term. There is no substitute for cash in the bank when a gale is blowing through world financial markets.

3. The results of highly-geared companies tend to exaggerate the underlying trend. All shareholders' funds are invested, and further substantial borrowings result in the company being fully committed and therefore subject to prevailing winds. When

businesses are recovering, high gearing can be a massive advantage for shareholders, but the reverse is also the case in tougher times.

It is difficult to set a firm guideline for gearing. Much depends on whether a company's borrowings are short or long-term, on the outlook for its industry and the efficiency of its management. Generally speaking, net gearing of over 50% calls for more detailed investigation. This is especially the case if a large proportion of the overall borrowings are short-term.

A comparison of a company's borrowings with the sector's composite figures can also be very revealing. The kinds of companies that tend to own their own properties are, for example, likely to be more highly geared than companies which do not require large premises, or prefer to rent their accommodation.

A company with a high dividend yield, low dividend cover and high gearing is often on the brink of trouble. That is why, in the tables of high-yielding shares, prominence has also been given to dividend cover and gearing.

Quick Ratio

The quick ratio is an attempt to indicate what would happen if a company suddenly had to pay off all its current liabilities. For this reason, only assets that can be readily turned into cash are included and stock and work-in-progress is excluded.

The basic formula is therefore:

$$\frac{\textit{Current assets less stock and work-in-progress}}{\textit{Current liabilities}} = \textit{quick ratio}$$

Generally speaking, I like to see a quick ratio of over one, but many retailing operations can manage on much less, as they can sell their products several weeks before paying their suppliers. Because of the vastly different circumstances of many businesses, the sectoral comparisons in the Tables Volume are most useful.

The trend is also important. If a company's quick ratio is low in relation to its peer group, and is declining rapidly, this can be a prelude to failure or to a fund-raising exercise.

Current Ratio

This ratio is determined by dividing the current assets of a business by its current liabilities. The resultant ratio shows the number of times current liabilities are covered by current assets.

The basic formula is therefore:

$$\frac{\textit{Current assets}}{\textit{Current liabilities}} = \textit{current ratio}$$

A high ratio (2 or more) is usually a sign of financial strength and a low ratio (1.25 or less) can be a sign of financial weakness.

Also, the year by year trend of current ratios can alert investors to fundamental changes in a business's financial structure. Retailing companies usually have small debtors, as most of their sales are paid for in cash; they therefore usually have lower than average current ratios. In other industries, large current ratios can sometimes result from excessive stocks or poor control of debtors.

Interest Cover

This ratio is calculated by taking a company's normalised historic profits *before interest and taxation* and dividing them by the annual interest charge. The resultant figure indicates the company's capacity to continue paying interest on its borrowings out of annual profits.

The basic formula is therefore:

$$\frac{\textit{Normalised profits before taxation and gross interest}}{\textit{Annual gross interest charge}} = \textit{Interest cover}$$

Low and/or deteriorating interest cover is an obvious danger signal and can sometimes be a precursor to a reconstruction, fund-raising or business failure.

Dividend cover

This ratio is calculated by taking a company's normalised historic earnings (or earnings per share) and dividing them by the net dividends payable (or net dividends per share). The resultant figure indicates the extent to which the historic dividend is covered by the company's earnings, ignoring any possible ACT consequences of a full distribution.

The basic formula is therefore:

$$\frac{\textit{Normalised historic earnings}}{\textit{Net dividends payable}} = \textit{Dividend cover}$$

or

$$\frac{\textit{EPS}}{\textit{Net dividends per share}} = \textit{Dividend cover}$$

Gearing, Cover

A company may have a high dividend yield, but poor cover will sound a warning signal that future dividend prospects are uncertain. In these circumstances, future earnings estimates should be studied carefully and special attention should be paid to the company's liquidity and gearing.

6

THE TABLES

The purpose of the REFS tables is to highlight anomalies, extremes and possible investment opportunities. The tables are based upon the up-to-date figures shown in the Companies Volume. Each set of tables focuses on a specific financial statistic.

The basic principles applied in the Tables Volume can be illustrated by the first table, which lists the companies most likely to be demoted from each index; a typical extract is shown below:

FT-SE 100 – INDEX DEMOTION CANDIDATES

Lowest market capitalisations.

			Share price (p)										
	Mkt Cap	1 Mo Rel	12 Months				Mkt Cap		5-Year Eps Growth	Prosp Eps Growth	Prosp	Prosp	
page	£m	Str %	High	Low	Recent	Company	£m	Prosp PER	Rate %	Rate %	PEG	DY %	PTBV
352	1,259	–20.9	£10.1	569	569	Amalgamated Packaging......	1,259	7.5	12.9	42.3	na	4.8	1.2
301	1,443	–3.5	160	135	140	Jones Group	1,443	12.2	1.7	8.5	1.4	4.9	4.2
150	1,523	–2.4	246	162	175	Williams Wholesale............	1,523	7.6	48.1	–36.7	na	6.2	0.9
287	1,538	–8.5	132	99.5	102	International Leisure...........	1,538	13.5	–19.0	13.7	1.0	5.1	1.4

Note: *Actual size is 50% larger than the example shown here.*

This table gives the shares in the FT-SE 100 Index with the lowest market capitalisations and therefore represents a list of the shares most likely to be demoted to the Mid 250 Index. The share with the lowest market capitalisation heads the list which continues in ascending order of market capitalisation to the next-most-likely share to be demoted, and so on.

The demotion table gives a good idea of the format in which information is laid out in most of the other tables. To the far left of each company name is the page number of that company's detailed entry in the Companies Volume, followed by five columns of market-related statistics:

	Mkt	1 Mo	Share price (p)			
	Cap	Rel	12 Months			
page	£m	Str %	High	Low	Recent	Company
352	1,259	-20.9	£10.1	569	569	Amalgamated Packaging......
301	1,443	-3.5	160	135	140	Jones Group ....
150	1,523	-2.4	246	162	175	Williams Wholesale............
287	1,538	-8.5	132	99.5	102	International Leisure............

The first of these is the market capitalisation of the company, followed by the share's relative strength during the last month, its 12 month high and low and the most recent price. Taken together, these statistics provide a clear picture of how the share is behaving in the market. The entry in the Companies Volume gives more comprehensive details, including a share-price graph and a record of highs and lows over five years.

To make the tables both familiar and easy to read, the format of the market-related statistics is *repeated throughout the REFS tables*. For the same reason, the first column to the right of the company name always shows the figure most pertinent to the purpose of the table. In the following example it is the market capitalisation:

Company	Mkt Cap £m	Prosp PER	5-Year Eps Growth Rate %	Prosp Eps Growth Rate %	Prosp PEG	Prosp DY %	PTBV
Amalgamated Packaging......	1,259	7.5	12.9	42.3	na	4.8	1.2
Jones Group	1,443	12.2	1.7	8.5	1.4	4.9	4.2
Williams Wholesale.............	1,523	7.6	48.1	–36.7	na	6.2	0.9
International Leisure............	1,538	13.5	–19.0	13.7	1.0	5.1	1.4

The five columns which follow the key statistic are common to many of the other tables and are presented in the same order whenever possible:

Prospective PER
5-year EPS growth rate %
Prospective EPS growth rate %
Prospective price-earnings growth factor
Prospective dividend yield %

The main exceptions to this order of presentation are tables which include one of the above five statistics as their main feature. For example, in the table of highest PERs, the PER is shown in the first right-hand column instead of the second. All the other statistics then follow in the usual order.

Alternative presentations are sometimes used because other statistics would be more illuminating or when statistics are placed next to each other for ease of comparison. For example, in the case of highest dividend yields, the prospective dividend yield is shown in the first right-hand column. This is then followed by dividend cover, because of its particular relevance. The PEG is dropped from the table as few high-yielders have one and more pertinent statistics for high-yielders, such as net gearing and price-to-cash flow, are shown instead.

There is usually space for one or two extra columns in the tables and these additional statistics will be shown on the far right. In the case of demotion candidates, there is only space for one extra column which is allocated to the price-to-tangible book value as a likely point of interest.

I will now review the tables one by one and explain their purpose and how the available extra column or columns have been allocated:

INDEX DEMOTION CANDIDATES

The importance of being in a major index is that it enhances both the reputation and stature of a company. In addition, and perhaps more importantly, tracker funds follow the indices, so demotion candidates will be sold heavily if their demotion is subsequently confirmed. It pays to be prescient!

The tables' statistics give a broad over-view of each candidate to enable investors to form their own view of the prospects for the company's share price. As mentioned earlier, the extra column has been devoted to price-to-tangible book value.

INDEX PROMOTION CANDIDATES

The same thinking in reverse applies to promotion candidates. Promoted shares tend to be bought heavily by tracker funds and other funds that restrict their investments to shares in the main indices.

You will notice that the market-capitalisation figures of many of the FT-SE Mid 250 and FT-SE SmallCap promotion candidates are followed by the letter 'R'. This indicates that they have been designated as reserves for promotion in the event that one or more constituents are deleted between quarterly reviews. They are shown in the tables in order of their reserve position.

Although market capitalisation is the main measure of a company's qualification for an index, there are others, so sometimes a few of the shares on the reserve list have lesser market capitalisations than some of the other shares in the tables. Companies without an 'R' are shown in descending order of market capitalisation.

As with demotion candidates, the final column has again been devoted to price-to-tangible book value.

HIGHEST RELATIVE STRENGTH

It is obviously of interest to know the best-performing shares in each of the indices each month. The first right-hand column therefore lists companies according to their relative strength over the past month. The second column shows relative strength over three months to enable the two figures to be compared easily.

The one-month relative strength table is very dynamic and up-to-date. It gives an early indication that something may be happening to a company even if it is not yet obvious from the fundamentals. Cross-checking the one-month relative strength figure with the three-month figure may provide further evidence that a new trend is developing.

LOWEST RELATIVE STRENGTH

Identifying shares showing poor relative strength in each of the indices is of crucial importance and may well give an early signal to cut a position. A quick check against the three-month relative strength figure may provide supporting evidence.

HIGHEST FUTURE GROWTH RATES FOR GROWTH COMPANIES

Again, this table is very dynamic as it is based on brokers' consensus estimates for the current and following year. The only companies that are included are those that REFS has deemed to be growth shares. They will therefore have PEGs and at least four years of consecutive EPS growth *either historic or forecast*. Because of this, many cyclicals and non-growth companies are not included in the tables. They also exclude some growth companies that have had a setback during the past two years.

As already explained, prospective normalised EPS, PERs, growth rates and PEGs are calculated by apportioning figures from the financial periods covered by brokers' estimates. *The aim is to show the rate of growth (and other statistics) for the 12 months immediately ahead. This makes all the figures in the tables both up-to-date and comparable.*

As growth is the key criterion, the prospective earnings growth rate appears in the first right hand column. Its normal position is taken by a column devoted to 3-year EPS growth rate to facilitate comparison with the 5-year and prospective growth rate figures. The last column has been used for ROCE which is always of interest with growth companies.

HIGHEST 3-YEAR GROWTH RATES

Exactly the same approach has been used as for the previous table except that the companies selected do not need to have at least four years' consecutive earnings growth either historic or forecast. In this table, the key criterion is EPS growth during the last three years. It is therefore not quite so up-to-date and dynamic as the table of highest future growth for growth companies. It is likely to highlight some of the same companies, but will also include some excellent growth companies whose prospects are not good enough to be highlighted in the highest future growth tables. The final two columns have been used for profit margin and ROCE.

HIGHEST 3-YEAR GROWTH RATES FOR GROWTH COMPANIES

The same approach as above except that the companies listed are restricted to growth companies within the REFS four-year definition. All entries will therefore have a PEG. The remaining two columns are again used for profit margin and ROCE.

HIGHEST 5-YEAR GROWTH RATES

These tables are very similar to the previous three. They are designed to show more consistent growth, although not all the companies are growth companies within the REFS four-year definition. In a few cases, future growth might be flagging a little. A key column to examine is the prospective EPS growth rate; if this remains buoyant and well above average, growth is obviously continuing. The final column has been used for ROCE.

HIGHEST 5-YEAR GROWTH RATES FOR GROWTH COMPANIES

These tables are similar to the previous four. All the selected companies are growth companies within the REFS four-year definition, so they all have a PEG. Again the final column has been used for ROCE.

HIGHEST PERs FOR GROWTH COMPANIES

In this table, the prospective PER is the key statistic. All the companies selected are growth companies within the REFS definition; they therefore also have a PEG.

Usually a high PER indicates that prospects for future EPS growth are excellent. Too high a PER can be a negative, especially if it is accompanied by a higher than average PEG. In such a case, the share price is demanding too much for future growth. However, sometimes a higher than average PER (and PEG) can be justified by the consistency of past growth and the reliability of future growth (which may also be accelerating).

To the right of the PER column, 5-year and 3-year EPS growth rates enable future growth to be compared with the past record. The PEG follows as a check on the price that is being demanded for that growth. The dividend yield is always of interest and the last column has been allocated to ROCE, always a key statistic for growth companies.

LOWEST PERs

Usually, a low prospective PER shows that a company has poor growth prospects. On occasions, the poor rating might be unjustified and the tables draw attention to companies that may have been neglected by the market. The key points to check immediately are the 5-year and 3-year EPS growth rates and, more particularly, the prospective EPS growth rate. If the company has a PEG it is worth special attention.

The remaining columns have been devoted to dividend yield and ROCE.

LOWEST PERs FOR GROWTH COMPANIES

This table is exactly the same as the previous one, but the only companies included are those that pass the REFS four-year test of EPS growth. The tables are therefore far more meaningful and should help to draw attention to neglected or under-valued growth shares.

The level of the PER is the key point for inclusion in the table, but close attention should be paid to the PEG as this is a more reliable measure of the price that is being paid for future growth.

LOWEST PEGs FOR GROWTH COMPANIES

In my view, these tables are the most useful for investors searching for attractive growth companies. The PEG is the clearest indicator of the price demanded for future growth. A low PEG is an obvious attraction and can be a strong buy signal for a share. However, be wary of using it in isolation - a very low figure can be an indication that a major problem lurks beyond the horizon.

Low PEGs usually arise in shares with very low PERs and above average growth prospects or relatively high PERs with exceptional growth prospects.

The prospective growth rate is followed by the 5-year and 3-year growth rate columns to help complete the picture. A negative figure in either of these columns can show that the company has had problems in the past and may be benefiting unduly from cyclical influences.

The ideal combination is a low PEG and a positive 5-year EPS growth rate with the prospective EPS growth rate at about the same level or better.

The last two columns have been used for prospective dividend yield and ROCE. With any companies of interest, reference should, of course, be made to the Companies Volume to double-check, in particular, the gearing, cash position, price-to-book value, price-to-cash flow and whether or not there have been any directors' dealings.

HIGHEST RETURNS ON CAPITAL EMPLOYED

A high return on capital employed is a validation of a company's competitive advantage and tends to be an attribute of growth companies. The first column shows the return on capital employed, based on the last annual report, and the second column shows the trend over the last five years. Be concerned if it is declining rapidly.

The prospective PER, five-year historic growth rate, prospective growth rate and prospective PEG (if applicable) are of obvious interest. The final column has been allocated to margin, which will, in most cases, be substantial. Companies with a high return on capital frequently also generate a high return on sales.

HIGHEST DIVIDEND YIELDS

All other things being equal, high-yielders tend to beat the market. This table highlights the shares with the highest dividend yields in each index.

The main worry about high-yielding shares is that the dividends may not be maintained. For this reason, the second column is devoted to prospective dividend cover and the last two columns to net gearing and price-to-cash flow.

Fragile dividend cover is an obvious reason for worry. Other causes for concern are net gearing of over 50% and/or a high price-to-cash flow ratio.

The ideal combination is a high and well-covered dividend yield, a modest PER, positive (even if negligible) 5-year growth, average to better-than-average future growth, modest or nil gearing and a low PCF. With any company of interest, reference should be made to the Companies Volume to double-check all the relevant statistics.

LOWEST PRICE-TO-TANGIBLE BOOK VALUE RATIOS

For investors interested in buying shares at a discount to asset value or near to asset value, these tables are of particular interest. It is important to note that the measure is a harsh one - all intangible assets, such as brand names, copyrights and trademarks, are treated as having a nil value. On occasions they can be very valuable indeed.

The PER, 5-year historic EPS growth rate, prospective EPS growth rate and prospective dividend yield are shown in the following columns. The price-to-sales ratio is then shown as this is often of particular interest with asset situations. The last column has been allocated to net gearing as excessive borrowings are often the reason for a company's share price standing at a discount to realisable value.

LOWEST PRICE-TO-CASH FLOW RATIOS

These tables highlight the companies which offer the most cash flow per share in relation to their share prices. All things being equal, a low PCF is a very positive investment factor.

The second column has been used for cash flow per share expressed in pence and the third for average cash flow per share over the last five years. The next two columns show the 5-year trend, and the net gearing taken from the last annual report. The last two columns have been allocated to the prospective PER and price-to-tangible book value.

The ideal company will have a low PCF, corroborated by a high average cash flow per share and a positive trend in cash flow. Net gearing will be moderate or nil, the prospective PER will be modest and the share price will be low in relation to tangible book value. Companies combining these characteristics are generating well-above-average cash every year and are of possible investment interest for that reason alone.

HIGHEST PERCENTAGE NET GEARING

Excessive gearing makes a company vulnerable during a liquidity crisis and also makes it very sensitive to changes in interest rates.

The net gearing figure measures total borrowings (less cash) as a percentage of shareholders' funds *including intangibles.* If intangibles were excluded there would be too many freakish figures in the tables.

The first column has been used for net gearing based on the last annual report and the second for gross gearing. The next four columns have been used for interest cover, dividend cover, the current ratio and PCF, all of which are particularly significant statistics for highly-leveraged companies. If interest and dividend cover is slim and the current ratio below 1.25, the company entry should be checked very thoroughly as, prima facie, the company has a problem.

Companies that are highly geared, even if they pass all the other tests, are likely to exaggerate market trends. Their shareholders' funds are fully invested and further borrowings result in the company being more committed and therefore more subject to prevailing winds. In times of recovery, high gearing can be a massive advantage to shareholders, but the reverse is also the case in tougher times.

The last column has been used for ROCE as shown by the last annual report. This is again a key figure for a company borrowing a lot of money. If the ROCE is less than the cost of borrowing, the company obviously has a major problem.

HIGHEST PERCENTAGE NET CASH

These tables show the companies with the highest percentages of cash (less borrowings) in relation to their shareholders' funds including intangibles.

The first column has been used for the percentage of cash shown by the last annual report and the second for the price-to-cash per share. The third column adds quoted investments to cash to give an idea of the potential cash position, even if some of the investments may not be readily realisable at all times.

The remaining four columns are devoted to net gearing, PCF, the prospective PER and the PTBV on the assumption that these statistics will be of particular interest to investors searching for asset situations.

HIGHEST PRICE-TO-SALES RATIOS

A high price-to-sales ratio is a potential negative for a share. Bio-tech companies and companies with new and developing products often feature at the top of the tables as they have very low sales to support their market capitalisations. Other companies that are likely to feature are those with branded or patented products with little competition and therefore very high margins.

The second column has been allocated to the trend of sales as, in many cases, turnover can be expanding very rapidly. The third and fourth columns have been used for margin and the trend of margins as these might be causes for concern if they are seen to be falling.

The fifth column has been used for the price-to-research ratio when applicable and the last two for prospective PER and PTBV.

Many fine companies will appear in these tables. Provided their sales continue to trend upwards and margins are maintained or improved, they should continue to go from strength to strength. However, a keen eye should be kept on these trends as, if they falter, the shares could be particularly vulnerable.

LOWEST PRICE-TO-SALES RATIOS

These tables are the converse of the previous ones. All other things being equal, shares with low PSRs are obviously better value than those with higher ratios. In companies with new management, a low PSR gives an idea of the future potential if margins can be improved.

The trend of both sales and margins is clearly of critical importance. The price-to-research ratio can also be very meaningful with technological companies. The PRR combines well with the PSR to give a measure of value when companies are losing money or have insignificant profits. At times like these, conventional measures such as the PER and PTBV are less useful.

The last two columns have been devoted to these two statistics to give an all-round picture.

LOWEST PRICE-TO-R & D EXPENDITURE RATIOS

The PRR is only a useful measure for companies which engage in a substantial amount of research and development expenditure every year. It can be a useful measure of value when companies are making losses or only insignificant profits. A low PRR can indicate that a very substantial amount is being spent on research in relation to the share price and that, in these terms alone, a share is a bargain.

The second and third columns have been devoted to PSR and the trend of sales because, as explained earlier, the PRR and PSR work in conjunction with each other. The fourth and fifth columns have been used for margins and trends and the last two for ROCE and prospective PER.

An important caveat on PRRs is that the allocation of research expenditure can be somewhat arbitrary; different companies may classify the same expenditure in different ways.

7

SECTOR LISTINGS

The sector listings enable you to get an instant fix on a company in relation to the market and in relation to the other members of its peer group. At a glance you can see, for example, how its prospective growth rate and PER compare with the market and the sector, if it has a low PEG or a high ROCE or if it is a bargain in terms of its PSR.

The constituents of each sector are shown in order of their market capitalisation. To the left of each table there are the usual market-related statistics, except for the 12-month highs and lows which have been deleted to provide extra space for more pertinent statistics. To the right of the company names are the usual financial measures such as prospective PER, 5-year EPS growth rate, prospective EPS growth rate, prospective PEG and prospective dividend yield.

Above the detailed figures for each company, you will find the market weighted average and market median together with the sector weighted average and the sector median. The weighted average is the result of weighting each statistic by the company's market capitalisation, whereas the median is the statistic at the midpoint of a table ranking all of the companies in the market or the sector by that statistic.

A look at the Electronic and Electrical Equipment sector in, for example, September 1994 brings this concept to life. General Electric, with a market capitalisation of nearly £8bn, dominates the sector, with BICC next at £1.34bn and then Delta at just over £700m. The last ten companies in the sector probably have a combined market capitalisation of under £50m.

It is not surprising, therefore, that the sector-weighted averages are, in most cases, very near to General Electric's figures, whereas the sector median can be very different. The key sector statistics like PSR, profit margin and ROCE show the position clearly:-

	Sector Weighted Average	**General Electric**	**Sector Median**
PSR	1.3	1.4	1.2
Profit Margin %	8.6	8.8	9.7
ROCE %	21.0	21.1	21.6

As you can see, the sector weighted average tends to hug the GEC figures, whereas the sector median tells a very different story.

It is also interesting to compare a sector's statistics with the market as a whole and with individual companies of interest. Take, for example, GEC in September 1994 in relation to popular investment measures like PER, dividend yield and prospective EPS growth rate:-

	PER	DY%	Prospective Growth Rate %
Market weighted average	15.2	4.4	14.8
Market median	13.9	4.0	14.2
Sector weighted average	14.5	4.4	13.8
Sector median	15.8	3.1	17.4
GEC	13.2	5.1	6.6

As you can see, the PER seems relatively attractive, but that is hardly surprising in view of the relatively poor prospective EPS growth rate. The dividend yield of 5.1% is very attractive and, because of GEC's high market capitalisation, lifts the sector weighted average well above the sector median.

The additional columns have been used for investment measures that are particularly pertinent to sector analysis:

1. Price-to-sales ratio
2. Profit margin
3. Return on capital employed

Growth companies often have high profit margins coupled with a high return on capital employed. Because of their high PERs (and consequently high share prices), they usually have high and therefore unattractive PSRs. Their managements make the most of existing sales and depend upon expansion for future growth. The trends of sales, margins and ROCE shown in the company entries are therefore of crucial importance.

Value investors will be more interested in companies with low PSRs. They are usually accompanied by miserable profit margins and a relatively poor ROCE. These kinds of companies are very prone to takeover or to a change of management. A more commercially-minded chief executive can often work wonders with such companies as was evidenced in recent years by Amersham International, Next and Eurotherm.

Shares that satisfy all one's investment criteria are hard to find. However, investment opportunities often hinge on just one very anomalous statistic, which can be identified by a detailed study of the sector listings.

Note:

The sector listings for Banks, Insurance, Life Assurance, Merchant Banks, Property and Other Financial are incomplete at present. We are working with specialists in these areas to determine the best use for all of the columns.

8

DIRECTORS' SHARE DEALINGS AND CEO CHANGES

DIRECTORS' SHARE DEALINGS

The individual entry for each company in the Companies Volume draws attention with a plus or minus sign to directors' dealings during the previous six months. In each monthly edition of the Tables Volume there is also a schedule of all significant directors' share dealings during the preceding six months.

An August 1993 study by Smith New Court demonstrated that by following directors' dealings an investor can outperform the market. There are a number of key points to consider when analysing directors' dealings:-

1. Directors' buying is a clearer signal than directors' selling. Directors decide to sell shares for a variety of reasons, such as buying a new house, to meet a tax obligation or simply to maintain a high standard of living. When a director buys a share, he or she is expressing the belief that the company's shares are a better

investment than cash. The director also usually believes that the share is under-valued.

The exceptions are when a director buys qualification shares on appointment, buys shares to take up an option that is expiring or when a director with a major shareholding buys a further trivial number of shares to excite interest in the company.

2. There is no doubt that there is comfort in numbers. Three or more directors buying a significant number of shares is a far more powerful indicator than an isolated transaction.

3. Directors' dealings need to be related to the number of shares already owned and the amount of money involved. The sale of 20,000 shares by a director owning one million shares worth £1 each is of no great significance. However, the sale of an entire shareholding of £20,000 worth of shares owned by a director can be a cause for alarm.

4. The identity of the buyer or seller of shares can be significant. The chairman, managing director or finance director are usually the three directors with the most intimate knowledge of a company's affairs. The transactions of other directors can be meaningful, but they are a little less likely to have the full story.

5. There are, of course, close periods when directors cannot sell shares. It is useful to know when they are, but I do not regard proximity to them as a particularly meaningful indicator.

Company REFS has been designed to pick up and highlight all of these factors. The monthly individual company entry shows with a minus if any directors have sold and with a plus if any have bought within the last six months. The figure before the plus or minus shows how many months ago the transaction took place.

Once alerted that there have been dealings, you should turn to the detailed list of director's dealings during the last six months. The list shows the position of the director, the director's residual shareholding after the sale or purchase and whether or not the transaction was linked to an option.

CHIEF EXECUTIVE OFFICER CHANGES

Details are given in each monthly edition of the Tables Volume of all chief executive officer changes during the preceding twelve months. The wording is taken from press releases which have to be read with a pinch of salt. Sometimes they are completely genuine but, on other occasions 'retirement from ill health' can mean 'judged incompetent by common acclaim' and 'wishes to reduce his executive responsibilities' is a polite way of saying 'he has done enough damage to the company already'.

The key point is that a new chief executive can herald the complete transformation of a company, especially if the executive in question is someone of high repute and the company is known to be mis-managed. There are many well-known precedents for very sizeable share-price gains in the years following this kind of change of chief executive.

The other side of the coin is that an executive of acknowledged great ability may leave a company without someone of comparable ability to replace him.

9

RESULTS ANNOUNCEMENTS, BROKERS' FORECAST CHANGES AND WARRANTS AND CONVERTIBLES

RESULTS ANNOUNCEMENTS

Details of all interim and preliminary announcements made during the previous month are given each month in the Tables Volume. They are in alphabetical order for ease of reference and their inclusion shows that they have been taken into account when compiling the company entries and tables.

BROKERS' FORECAST CHANGES

Details of brokers' consensus forecast changes during the month are given in the Tables Volume on an index-by-index basis. The forecasts are shown in two columns - the current and following year. In both cases, the change during the month and the last three months is highlighted. Clearly it pays to be alert to downwards or upwards forecast changes that seem to be part of a trend. A downwards revision during the previous month may be a further extension of a reduction during the preceding three. This could be the beginning of adverse news-flow which can be very damaging to a company's market rating.

The next two columns show the relative strength during the preceding month and last three months. The market's reaction to upwards or downwards revisions of forecasts is usually the best indicator of whether or not the news is a surprise.

The final columns are devoted to the PER and the prospective growth rate, adjusted to take account of the most recent consensus forecast.

WARRANTS AND CONVERTIBLES

Company REFS intends to supply details of all warrants and convertibles for all quoted and USM companies, excluding investment trusts. These statistics will give exact details of conversion terms to supply a complete picture of possible future dilution and to focus attention on alternative ways of making an equity investment in the companies in question.

10

USING COMPANY REFS

Company REFS is designed to facilitate share selection and also the regular monthly review of a portfolio of shares.

Most investors use a 'top down' or 'bottom up' approach to identify a potential investment. *Company REFS* helps to meet both objectives.

'TOP DOWN' INVESTING

For 'top down' investors, the Tables Volume and, in particular, the general and sector tables are the obvious ways to spot interesting investments. You might be on the lookout for companies with, for example, low PEGs, high dividend yields, substantial asset backing or a higher-than-average return on their capital employed. The tables instantly highlight the top 25 companies satisfying your particular criteria in each of the indices and outside them.

Similarly, you might feel that a particular sector has very attractive long-term prospects. The sector tables give you a complete picture of all the companies in a sector and how their financial statistics compare with the averages of the market as a whole, the sector and each and every company within it. Once you have identified a few companies that meet your criteria, simply turn to the individual company entry in the Companies Volume to obtain much more detailed information.

'BOTTOM UP' INVESTING

For 'bottom up' investors, the individual company entries in the Companies Volume are the first port of call. After analysis, any company of interest can be put in context by referring to the Tables Volume.

Note: *Actual size is 50% larger than the example shown here.*

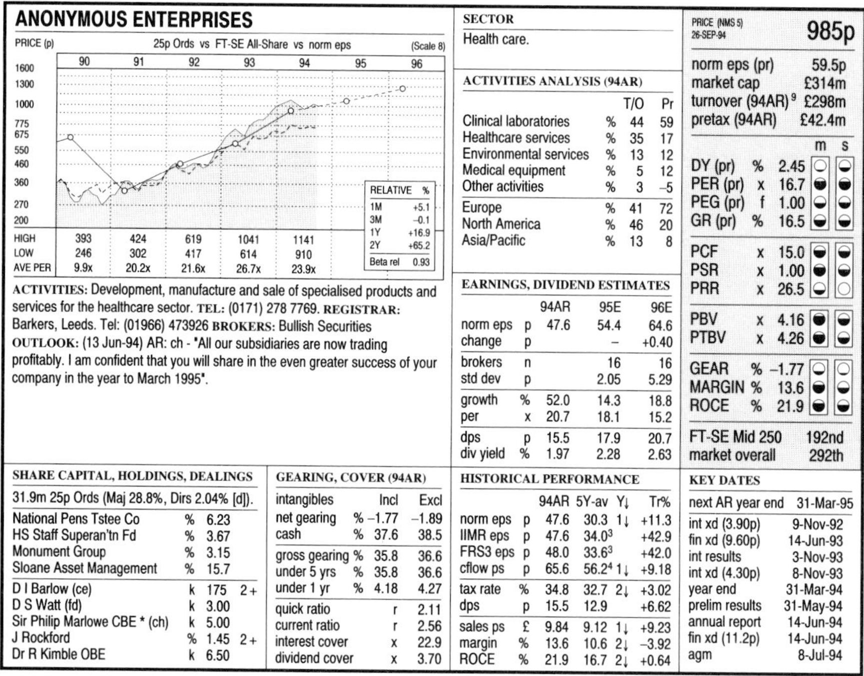

ANONYMOUS ENTERPRISES

PRICE (p) 25p Ords vs FT-SE All-Share vs norm eps (Scale 8)

	90	91	92	93	94	95	96
HIGH	393	424	619	1041	1141		
LOW	246	302	417	614	910		
AVE PER	9.9x	20.2x	21.6x	26.7x	23.9x		

RELATIVE	%
1M	+5.1
3M	−0.1
1Y	+16.9
2Y	+65.2
Beta rel	0.93

ACTIVITIES: Development, manufacture and sale of specialised products and services for the healthcare sector. **TEL:** (0171) 278 7769. **REGISTRAR:** Barkers, Leeds. Tel: (01966) 473926 **BROKERS:** Bullish Securities **OUTLOOK:** (13 Jun-94) AR: ch - "All our subsidiaries are now trading profitably. I am confident that you will share in the even greater success of your company in the year to March 1995".

SECTOR

Health care.

ACTIVITIES ANALYSIS (94AR)

		T/O	Pr
Clinical laboratories	%	44	59
Healthcare services	%	35	17
Environmental services	%	13	12
Medical equipment	%	5	12
Other activities	%	3	−5
Europe	%	41	72
North America	%	46	20
Asia/Pacific	%	13	8

EARNINGS, DIVIDEND ESTIMATES

		94AR	95E	96E
norm eps	p	47.6	54.4	64.6
change	p		–	+0.40
brokers	n		16	16
std dev	p		2.05	5.29
growth	%	52.0	14.3	18.8
per	x	20.7	18.1	15.2
dps	p	15.5	17.9	20.7
div yield	%	1.97	2.28	2.63

PRICE (NMS 5) 26-SEP-94 **985p**

norm eps (pr)	59.5p
market cap	£314m
turnover (94AR)[9]	£298m
pretax (94AR)	£42.4m

			m	s
DY (pr)	%	2.45		
PER (pr)	x	16.7		
PEG (pr)	f	1.00		
GR (pr)	%	16.5		
PCF	x	15.0		
PSR	x	1.00		
PRR	x	26.5		
PBV	x	4.16		
PTBV	x	4.26		
GEAR	%	−1.77		
MARGIN	%	13.6		
ROCE	%	21.9		

FT-SE Mid 250	192nd
market overall	292th

SHARE CAPITAL, HOLDINGS, DEALINGS

31.9m 25p Ords (Maj 28.8%, Dirs 2.04% [d]).

National Pens Tstee Co	%	6.23	
HS Staff Superan'tn Fd	%	3.67	
Monument Group	%	3.15	
Sloane Asset Management	%	15.7	
D I Barlow (ce)	k	175	2+
D S Watt (fd)	k	3.00	
Sir Philip Marlowe CBE * (ch)	k	5.00	
J Rockford	%	1.45	2+
Dr R Kimble OBE	k	6.50	

GEARING, COVER (94AR)

intangibles		Incl	Excl
net gearing	%	−1.77	−1.89
cash	%	37.6	38.5
gross gearing	%	35.8	36.6
under 5 yrs	%	35.8	36.6
under 1 yr	%	4.18	4.27
quick ratio	r		2.11
current ratio	r		2.56
interest cover	x		22.9
dividend cover	x		3.70

HISTORICAL PERFORMANCE

		94AR	5Y-av	Y↓	Tr%
norm eps	p	47.6	30.3	1↓	+11.3
IIMR eps	p	47.6	34.0[3]		+42.9
FRS3 eps	p	48.0	33.6[3]		+42.0
cflow ps	p	65.6	56.2[4]	1↓	+9.18
tax rate	%	34.8	32.7	2↓	+3.02
dps	p	15.5	12.9		+6.62
sales ps	£	9.84	9.12	1↓	+9.23
margin	%	13.6	10.6	2↓	−3.92
ROCE	%	21.9	16.7	2↓	+0.64

KEY DATES

next AR year end	31-Mar-95
int xd (3.90p)	9-Nov-92
fin xd (9.60p)	14-Jun-93
int results	3-Nov-93
int xd (4.30p)	8-Nov-93
year end	31-Mar-94
prelim results	31-May-94
annual report	14-Jun-94
fin xd (11.2p)	14-Jun-94
agm	8-Jul-94

The tables rank companies in relation to particular investment criteria or within their sector. Also shown in this volume is whether directors have dealt recently or if a convertible or warrant offers a better way of investing in the company. All of these facts and many more are readily available in the Tables Volume.

All investment analysts have their own investment beliefs, preferences and particular way of analysing an investment. I will demonstrate my approach with a hypothetical company entry (see opposite) and show how I decide whether or not the share in question is a worthwhile candidate for my portfolio.

First, I glance at the graph. It gives an overview and a visual impression of recovery followed by growth, taking EPS over the 1990 high. Also, it shows that in 1995 and 1996 EPS growth is forecast to continue at a strong rate. The present PER of 16.7 compares favourably with the average PER for the share from 1991 onwards. However, it is on the high side for the sector, as evidenced by the moons in the key statistics.

The relative strength has been very good over the last two years, although recently it seems to be tailing off. However, the outlook statement is clearly bullish and I see from the EARNINGS, DIVIDEND ESTIMATES panel that 16 brokers anticipate 14.3% growth in 1995 and 18.8% is forecast for 1996. So far so good.

A quick look at the SHARE CAPITAL panel tells me who the major shareholders are and shows what the directors have been doing with their shares. Good news - the chief executive bought some shares two months ago and so did another director. No entry in CHIEF EXECUTIVE OFFICER CHANGES confirms that there has not been a change of chief executive during the last 12 months. I examine DIRECTORS SHARE DEALINGS in the Tables Volume to confirm that the chief executive's share purchase was not trivial. He bought 25,000 for £245,000, adding to his present holding of 150,000 shares.

Now to check the GEARING, COVER panel. I dislike companies laden with debt. Good news again - gross gearing is matched by a strong cash position.

A more detailed survey of the key statistics tells me that the market capitalisation is £314m - a nice size, with plenty of scope for future growth, 192nd in the FT-SE Mid 250 Index. However, even if growth continues with an occasional acquisition, it will be some years before the company becomes a candidate for promotion to the FT-SE 100 Index.

The 12-months-ahead PER of 16.7 is high, but not excessive for a company with a 16.5% growth rate. The PEG of 1.00 reflects this. Another look at the sector tables confirms that the PEG is attractive - the average PEG for the market as a whole is 1.5 on a weighted-average basis, the sector-weighted average is 1.4 and the sector median 1.2.

The PCF at 15.0 is lower than the PER which is superficially a good sign and about average for the market and the sector. A quick check of the HISTORICAL PERFORMANCE panel reveals that cash flow is strong and on a rising trend. The nil net gearing position is also comforting.

The PSR at 1.00 is average for the sector. The PRR of 26.5 is also very similar to several other companies in its industry. (PRR information is sporadic so I usually check the PRR of a company against major comparable companies in the industry on a company-by-company basis. I also check the PRR tables to see if the company is in the top ten in its index.)

The price-to-book value is 4.16, which is about average for its sector. There are very few intangibles so PTBV is nearly the same.

A margin of 13.6% seems reasonable, but slightly low for the sector. Also the HISTORICAL PERFORMANCE panel shows that margins have been narrowing, although they are still well above the five-year average. Perhaps sales are being expanded at the expense of margins. The same panel confirms that sales per share have been growing at 9.2% per annum with only one down year. I must bear narrowing margins in mind when reading the chairman's statement and the company's annual report and try to pin down the reasons more accurately.

ROCE of 21.9% is excellent although it is about the same as the sector average. The trend is up slightly and the current figure is well above the five-year average.

Now I take a really detailed look at the company's ACTIVITIES. Clinical laboratories and health care are the two main activities, accounting for 79% of turnover. Clinical laboratories is clearly more profitable.

The geographical analysis is interesting. 46% of turnover in North America produces only 20% of profits. Continental Europe shows the opposite picture. Almost certainly it is in North America where margins are deteriorating.

Another look at the EARNINGS, DIVIDEND ESTIMATES panel to check the consensus of brokers' forecasts. Good to see the 1996 consensus estimate revised upwards. Above-average growth of 14.3% is forecast for 1995 and 18.8% for 1996. Standard deviation of 2.05p about 4% of forecast EPS of 54.4p - nothing to worry about in 1995. 5.29p in 1996 probably means the net difference for 1996 is 3.24p (5.29p - 2.05p), which is only 5%.

15% dividend increases are forecast for both 1995 and 1996. Although the present yield is well below average, the GEARING, COVER panel confirms that it is well covered.

The HISTORICAL PERFORMANCE panel confirms that the normalised, IIMR and FRS3 EPS are almost the same. Usually a good sign - no exceptional items.

Cash flow per share is healthily above EPS and on a rising trend. The tax charge is a full one, so there should be no nasty surprises (like running out of tax losses available for set-off) coming from that source. Only margins appear to be in a negative five-year trend.

With an above-average growth rate, below-average PEG and good liquidity, the share is a potential buy, subject to more detailed information on declining margins.

Now I examine the KEY DATES to see when the next results are due and also the date of the last AGM. I need to see the most recent detailed accounts and read a few brokers' circulars and all relevant press comment to get a complete feel for the company. However, first I check the Tables Volume again to see if the company features in any of the Mid 250 Index tables. I quickly find that it is one of the top 25 companies in terms of 5-year and 3-year growth rates, but it misses by just two decimal points the table of 25 lowest PEGs in the Mid 250 Index.

I always turn to the sector tables to get an instant fix on a company in relation to the market and other members of its peer group. All the statistics for the company except margin compare favourably with other companies in the sector. Its 13.6% compares with a sector median of 14.5%, which is OK unless margins continue to narrow.

The PER deserves special attention because the sector-weighted average of 24.5 is distorted by the results of one company which has just recovered from losses and has a PER of over 150. In this kind of case, the sector median PER of 14.4 is far more meaningful and this compares with the company's PER of 16.7. However, as already indicated, the growth rate (excluding the statistical anomaly referred to above) is the highest in its sector and the PEG is out of line and very attractive.

Directors' dealings are always worth double-checking again in detail and so are chief executive officer changes and consensus forecast changes. In the latter case, there was only an upward revision of the 1996 estimate. Frequent downward revisions are always worrying as adverse news-flow can be the worst possible influence on a share price.

The SHARE CAPITAL, HOLDINGS panel makes it clear that there are no convertibles or warrants in issue. If there were, I would examine the terms in the Tables Volume to see if any of them offered a better way of investing in the company.

PORTFOLIO REVIEW

Another invaluable use of *Company REFS* is for portfolio reviews. Every month it is well worthwhile to review each and every share in your portfolio to see if there has been a major change that may have gone unnoticed on a more day-to-day basis.

My first thought is to check the relative strength during the previous month. If this is poor, I then check the last three months and the last year. A quick look at the OUTLOOK indicates whether there has been any price-sensitive announcement.

The EARNINGS, DIVIDEND ESTIMATES panel is like a scout looking for an oasis or possible trouble beyond the immediate horizon. Upward or downward revisions to the estimates of future EPS are shown under 'change'. Downward revisions are obviously worrying, especially if they are accompanied by poor relative strength during the month. This is usually enough to persuade me to sell immediately.

The SHARE CAPITAL, HOLDINGS panel tells you immediately if any of the directors have been buying or selling any shares. Institutional dealings are also of interest, especially if a really major shareholder has begun to lessen its stake and might have many more shares left to sell. Exact details of the last six months directors' dealings are set out in the Tables Volume.

The other sensitive indicator to watch closely is the PEG which will show if the shares are becoming too expensive. This would especially be the case if there were a major downward revision of future estimates as this would raise the prospective PER and lower the future growth rate, compounding into a much higher and much less attractive PEG.

The other key statistics, such as net gearing, should also be quickly scanned to make sure that there has been no major change during the month.

Finally, I turn to the Tables Volume to see if my shares have had a major change of position during the month. Sometimes, changes are imperceptible on a day-to-day basis, so I like to make sure, for example, that their PERs are not creeping into the high end of the tables - a sign that they are becoming the darlings of the market.

I also have a close look at each of my shares in the appropriate sector tables. Although I usually know what is happening to my portfolio, I am sometimes unaware of a gradual change taking place in a sector as a whole. I like to review my shares regularly in their natural context (ie their sector) to get a fix on their relative attractions.

CONCLUSION

The final section of this guide book is a Technical Appendix which has been prepared by Chris Cole of Hemmington Scott. He explains in detail the presentation and basis of calculating all the statistics used in *Company REFS.*

I hope that you will find that *Company REFS* soon becomes an indispensible addition to your investment armoury. We are anxious to continue to improve and develop the product, so if you have any suggestions, please write with full details to Hemmington Scott.

TECHNICAL APPENDIX

TABLE OF CONTENTS

1

GENERAL

A. READERS' QUERIES AND COMMENTS

Company REFS was designed with the help and advice of some of the UK's most successful professional and private investors; the presentation and basis of calculation of each statistic has been carefully formulated to meet their requirements. Whilst we are confident that *Company REFS* will meet your investment needs, we welcome any comments which can help us to develop and further improve the product.

Queries or comments should be addressed to:

Hemmington Scott Publishing Limited,
City Innovation Centre,
26-31 Whiskin Street,
London EC1R 0BP

Tel: 0171-278-7769 Fax: 0171-278-9808

B. COMPILATION AND SOURCES

Coverage

Companies must comply with the following criteria for inclusion within the Companies section:

- Have equity shares listed on the London Stock Exchange, with either a full or USM listing (as indicated)
- Be registered in the United Kingdom, and report in Sterling
- **Not** be trading as an Investment Trust

Around 1,600 companies currently meet these criteria.

Investment trusts

Investment trusts are not included within *Company REFS* except as required to ensure the accurate positioning of each company within its index, and within the market overall. The index ranking (e.g. FT-SE 100 - 58th) shows the current position of the company within its index, after ranking all fellow constituents (including any investment trusts) according to their latest market capitalisation. Similarly, investment trusts are taken into account for the overall market ranking, and also appear within the summary of index promotion and demotion candidates in the companion tables volume.

In all other respects, investment trusts are outside the scope of *Company REFS*. They do not appear as individual entries nor within the remaining tables.

Banks and insurance companies
These are included within *Company REFS*, but certain figures and calculations are not relevant, and are therefore not shown. These include gearing, turnover, margin and ROCE (return on capital employed).

Sources
The information published in *Company REFS* is derived from the Hemmington Scott Corporate Information Database, which is maintained using information drawn from primary sources, mainly the company's own annual reports and interim statements. This is supplemented with information officially announced by the company through the Stock Exchange, including preliminary results, board changes, notifiable changes to director and major shareholdings, and price-sensitive information regarding trading conditions, bids, offers or deals.

Consensus earnings forecasts are supplied by Earnings Guide Ltd.

C. *PRODUCTION CYCLE AND TIMELINESS*

The production of *Company REFS* is scheduled for publication on the first Friday of each month. In normal circumstances, it is compiled using information available up to the close of business on the Monday of the same week, including share prices. If the markets do not trade that day, for example on a public holiday, then prices for the previous trading day are used.

D. *NOTIONAL DILUTION*

If the future conversion of other classes of share capital or debt will cause a potential dilution of earnings per ordinary share, *Company REFS* shows historic earnings per share (EPS) on a fully-diluted basis.

Any statistic or calculation which incorporates, or invites comparison with, historic EPS is also presented on a fully-diluted basis. Those statistics affected include:

- historic and forecast EPS
- historic cash flow per share
- prospective price-earnings ratio (PER)
- price-earnings growth factor (PEG)
- historic and forecast EPS growth

Calculations based on full dilution notionally assume that any future share issues, which could take place upon conversion of other classes of debt or share capital, have already occurred. This can involve adjusting earnings as well as increasing the actual number of shares. Adjustments to earnings can reflect, for example, a lower dividend or interest payout (as with convertible fixed dividend securities or debt), or a notional increase in earnings capacity through a larger capital base (as with options or warrants to subscribe for ordinary shares).

E. *ENHANCED SCRIP DIVIDENDS*

A number of companies offer an enhanced scrip option as an alternative to paying shareholders a cash dividend. Within *Company REFS*, the existence of such an option is not at present noted, nor is any retrospective adjustment factor applied.

F. *PROFIT WARNINGS*

The announcement of a 'profit warning' is regarded as rendering out of date (pending revisions) any existing forecasts. Until revised forecasts are available, the key statistics (in the shaded panel on the right-hand side of the company entry) are shown on a historic basis, and the caption 'now awaiting updated brokers' estimates for this company' is temporarily displayed within the 'Earnings, Dividend Estimates' panel.

G. *CHANGES OF YEAR-END*

Companies occasionally change their financial year-end, for example from 31st December to 31st March, so that the accounting period reported is of a non-standard length - either 3 months or 15 months in this example.

With two specific exceptions described below, all figures shown within *Company REFS*, and any comparisons or trends, are automatically adjusted to an 'annualised' basis. Therefore changes of year-end are not specifically highlighted within *Company REFS*. If a forthcoming change in year end is notified, this is reflected, within the panel of Key Dates, when the date shown for 'next AR year-end' ceases to be the anniversary of the previous year-end.

The only two figures which are exceptions to this rule, and which are NOT annualised, are the last reported turnover and pre-tax profit shown in the shaded panel of Key Statistics on the right hand side of each company entry. When these figures relate to a non-standard period, a superscript indicates the duration of the accounting period in months - e.g. 3 or 15 in the above example.

2

KEY STATISTICS

A. USE OF SUFFIXES

pr (prospective):
Whenever broker forecasts are available for prospective earnings and dividends these are incorporated to provide, as far as possible, a rolling 12 months-ahead view within the following key statistics:

norm EPS	(Normalised earnings per share)
DY	(Dividend yield)
PER	(Price-earnings ratio)
PEG	(Price-earnings growth factor)
GR	(Earnings growth rate)

The following example shows the calculation of 12 months-ahead EPS for a hypothetical company, measured at 31st May 1994. Its next year-end is 31st December 1994, and earnings forecasts are available for the current year (to December 1994) and following year (to December 1995).

	Year end 31 Dec 93 (Historic)	Year end 31 Dec 94 (Forecast)	Year end 31 Dec 95 (Forecast)
EPS	15.7p	18.5p	21.0p
Apportionment:	n/a	7 months	5 months
Apportioned EPS:	n/a	10.8p	8.7p
12 months-ahead EPS (1 Jun 94 to 31 May 95)		19.5p	

Where the 'pr' suffix is absent, the statistics are based solely on historic data.

94AR (Annual Report) or
94PA (Preliminary Announcement):
The number (e.g. 93, 94 etc.) refers to the last reported period according to the calendar year in which it ended; the suffix denotes the source, being either the Annual Report ('AR'), or a Preliminary Announcement ('PA'). The precise date of the period end is shown in the 'KEY DATES' panel.

B. PRICE

The price shown is the mid-market price at the close of business on the date given alongside. This is the latest possible date which internal production schedules will allow and, in ideal circumstances, is the Monday preceding the first Friday in each month. This date may, if necessary, be the nearest previous trading day.

C. MAJOR EVENT FLAG

A flag draws attention to specific major events which have recently occurred. The following major events are flagged:

'R' - Rights issue: a rights issue, or open offer, is currently in progress

'S' - Suspension: shares are currently suspended from trading

'T' - Takeover: the company is making, or has received, a takeover offer

The major event flag is set when one of the above situations pertains at the latest production cut-off date. This is normally the Monday preceding the first Friday in the month of publication shown on the front cover. The date and nature of the event are provided in a note appended to the textual information beneath the share price graph.

D. NMS (NORMAL MARKET SIZE)

Normal Market Size indicates, in thousands, the average trading quantity for the stock. For example, 'NMS 5' indicates that the average market trade is 5,000 shares. A stock's NMS is directly related to its liquidity. The higher the number, the more liquid the stock.

Liquidity is a measure of the amount of market turnover, and represents share trading volume multiplied by the price at which each trade takes place.

NMS bands are allocated by the Stock

Exchange acccording to a formula based on a) the total trading volume of each stock over the past 12 months and b) the closing mid-market price. The NMS band for each stock is allocated at the end of each quarter, and published one month later. The NMS bands, and the ranges they represent, are as follows:

NMS band (000's)	Share range equivalent
0.5	0 - 667
1	668 - 1,333
2	1,334 - 2,400
3	2,401 - 3,750
5	3,751 - 6,667
10	6,668 - 12,000
15	12,001 - 18,000
25	18,001 - 33,000
50	33,001 - 60,000
75	60,001 - 93,000
100	93,001 - 160,000
200	over 160,000

The formula applied is as follows:

$$\frac{\text{Value of market turnover in previous 12 months (£)}}{\text{Closing mid-market price on last day of qtr} \times 10{,}000} = NMS$$

Example:

Stock - *XYZ PLC Ord.*

Market turnover value (previous 12 months) - *£2,142.72m*

Closing mid-market price - *312p*

$$NMS = \frac{2,142,720,000}{3.12 \times 10,000} = 68,677 \text{ shares}$$

NMS band = 75,000

NMS bands are allocated in order to determine the cut-off point at which all deals in a stock must immediately be published on SEAQ, the Stock Exchange Automated Quotation system used by market traders. Similarly, they determine which deals are subject to publication on SEAQ after a 90 minute delay (essentially very large ones), and those for which publication does not occur at all on SEAQ (essentially very small ones).

All SEAQ stocks with an NMS of 2,000 shares or more (about 900 stocks) have immediate trade publication on SEAQ for all trades up to three times their NMS. Trades in these stocks larger than three times NMS are published after a 90 minute delay. Trades in these stocks larger than 75 times NMS can optionally be published under a block trade facility; this enables a market-maker to unwind 90% of his position over a maximum of five business days before publication takes place.

No trade publication occurs on SEAQ for trades in stocks with an NMS of 500 or 1,000 shares (about 1,200 stocks). These are considered to be much less liquid and publication of these trades appears the next day in SEDOL (the Stock Exchange Daily Official List). The only exceptions are agency cross trades, and all trades in stocks which are in a bid situation, both of which are published immediately on SEAQ regardless of the stock's NMS.

E. NORM EPS (NORMALISED EARNINGS PER SHARE)

Earnings are based on estimated future results if available, in which case the forecasts are apportioned to give a rolling 12 months-ahead view, and the suffix 'pr' is used to indicate prospective. Otherwise reported historic results are used, adjusted to a 'normalised' basis to achieve a sound comparison with future estimates.

When the EPS is historic, the result is initially calculated by dividing the earnings by the weighted average number of shares in issue during the year.

Historic EPS
Normalised historic EPS are calculated as follows:

Step 1:

	profit after tax
-	minority interest
-	preference dividends
=	reported earnings (unadjusted)

Step 2:

	reported earnings	
+	non-trading losses	*net of tax and minority interest adjustments*
+	exceptional charges	
-	non-trading profits	
-	exceptional income	
=	normalised earnings	

Step 3:

$$\frac{\textit{normalised earnings (£)}}{\textit{weighted average share in issue}} \times \textit{100p} = \textit{normalised EPS (p)}$$

Forecast EPS
When based on forecasts, EPS is initially the result of dividing the consensus of brokers' forecast earnings by the current number of shares in issue. The consensus is taken as the average, or arithmetic mean, of all the individual contributing brokers' views.

Adjustments
The figures for both earnings and the number of shares can be subject to adjustment for a variety of reasons which fall into the following four categories:

1. Non-trading and exceptional profits/losses.
The forecast results almost certainly exclude the effect of any future exceptional or non-trading events. Because of this, the reported earnings are adjusted to a normalised basis. This provides a realistic base against which EPS estimates for the following two periods can be compared, and EPS growth can be measured. Normalised earnings have been calculated by excluding any exceptional or non-trading profits and losses. The methodology is fully explained on page 144 under the heading: Calculation of IIMR Headline and normalised earnings.

2. Share capital changes.
If a change in share capital gives rise to a share price adjustment factor, the factor is applied to restore comparability between EPS figures from different time periods. Examples include rights issues, scrip issues, and share consolidations or subdivisions.

3. Annualisation.
Adjustments to annualise the last reported EPS are necessary when the period is greater or less than 12 months in duration. The methodology is fully explained on page 149 under the heading: Adjustments to figures, ratios and per share values.

4. Notional dilution.
EPS is shown on a fully-diluted basis. This notionally assumes that any known future possible share issues, which would take place upon conversion of other classes of debt or share capital, have already occurred. Additional adjustments are also made to reflect, for example, lower dividend or interest payouts, or an increased earnings capacity through a larger capital base.

F. MARKET CAP (MARKET CAPITALISATION)

This is the market value of the total equity share capital, including all classes of ordinary shares, and excluding preference shares and convertibles. Market capitalisation is based on the latest share price available prior to publication.

It is calculated by multiplying the number of ordinary shares in issue by the latest share price.

G. TURNOVER

This is the latest available reported figure for turnover, or sales. The suffix indicates the calendar year in which the last period ended (e.g. 93, or 94 etc.) and the source (either Preliminary Announcement or Annual Report). Turnover excludes sales taxes, government levies, excise duty, and VAT.

The turnover shown is over the duration of the actual reporting period, and the presence of a superscript (e.g. 15 or 9) indicates the number of months of any non-standard period. Note that the figure is *not* annualised.

H. PRE-TAX (PROFIT)

This is the latest available figure for unadjusted reported pre-tax profit. The suffix indicates the calendar year in which the last period ended (e.g. 93, or 94 etc.) and the source (either Preliminary Announcement or Annual Report).

The pre-tax profit shown is over the duration of the actual reporting period, and the presence of a superscript (e.g. 15 or 9) indicates the number of months of any non-standard period. Note that the figure is *not* annualised.

I. MARKET AND SECTOR 'MOONS'

For each statistic where a result is calculated, the moons provide an instant visual indication of its position relative to:

- all other companies in *Company REFS* (the Market moons in the left-hand column)
- all other companies within the same sector (the Sector moons in the right-hand column)

The relative position is fixed by ranking all the companies in the market, or sector, for which that statistic is calculated, with the highest values placed at the top. The relative position within this ranking directly determines the relative position of the horizontal line within the circle. The highest value is represented by a full or black circle, and the lowest by an empty or clear circle. If, for example, a statistic is ranked sixth highest out of eight, the circle is calibrated to be exactly one quarter full.

'Not applicable' is indicated when the circle contains crossed vertical and horizontal lines.

J. DY (DIVIDEND YIELD)

If consensus brokers' estimates are available, the dividend yield is based on dividend forecasts for the next two reported periods; these are apportioned to give a rolling 12 months-ahead view using the latest share price, and the suffix 'pr' is used to indicate prospective. The 12 months-ahead calculation is illustrated on page 118 under the heading 'Use of Suffixes'. In the absence of brokers' estimates, reported historic dividends are used in calculating the yield.

The dividend yield expresses the annual dividend of a share as a percentage return on investment at the prevailing market price. The net dividend for the period, whether historic or forecast, is grossed up by the appropriate rate of income tax and expressed as a percentage of the latest share price. The net dividend is subject to adjustment where the share capital or year end may have changed.

Where a dividend yield is historic, it shows the annualised dividend for the last reported period as a percentage of the latest share price.

The calculation of dividend yield is performed as follows:

Step 1:

For the purpose of illustration, it is assumed that the standard rate of income applicable to dividends declared net is 20%. On this basis, it follows that the net dividend per share is 80% of its gross value. The grossed-up dividend per share is therefore calculated as follows:

$$\text{net dividend per share} \times \frac{100}{(100\text{-}20)} = \text{gross dividend per share}$$

Step 2:

$$\frac{\text{gross dividend per share}}{\text{latest share price}} \times 100 = DY\ (\%)$$

K. PER (PRICE-EARNINGS RATIO)

The PER expresses the current share price as a multiple of the normalised earnings per share figure described on page 119 under 'Norm EPS'. The PERs are calculated using the latest price shown in the top right-hand corner of the entry.

EPS are based on estimated future results if available, in which case forecasts for the next two reported periods are apportioned to give a rolling 12 months-ahead view, and the suffix 'pr' is used to indicate prospective. Otherwise reported historic results are used, adjusted to a normalised basis in order to achieve a sound comparison with future estimates. The calculation of 12 months-ahead EPS is illustrated on page 118 under the heading: Use of suffixes.

The calculation is as follows:

$$\frac{\textit{latest share price}}{\textit{normalised EPS}} = \textit{PER (x)}$$

L. PEG (PRICE-EARNINGS GROWTH FACTOR)

The PEG factor measures the relative cost of earnings growth at the current share price. It is therefore only relevant to those companies which can truly be considered to have growth shares.

The PEG factor is simply the price-earnings ratio (PER) divided by the earnings growth rate (GR), as follows:

$$\frac{\textit{PER}}{\textit{GR}} = \textit{PEG factor}$$

The calculation of each element is explained under separate headings (see above for 'PER' and below for 'GR').

The REFS definition of 'growth' companies
A PEG is only calculated where a company meets all of the following criteria:

- there must be continuous growth in normalised EPS for four consecutive periods (including any available forecasts)
- each of the last five normalised results must be positive (i.e. none may show a loss)
- where four periods of growth follow a previous setback, it must have achieved, or be expected to achieve, its highest normalised EPS (whether historic or forecast) in the latest period out of the last six

For recently listed shares, the consecutive periods may include figures based on information taken from listing prospectuses.

(NOTE: PEGs are not calculated for companies in the Property or Building & Construction sectors.)

M. GR (EARNINGS GROWTH RATE)

Growth refers to the rate of increase in normalised EPS and is measured, when possible, on a rolling 12 months-ahead basis. Normalised EPS is explained on page 119 under the heading 'Norm EPS'.

The suffix '(pr)' indicates that earnings forecasts are available and have been used in calculating the prospective growth rate; otherwise growth refers solely to the rate of increase in historic normalised EPS.

Calculating the growth rate for each period (historic or forecast)
For each period, whether historic or forecast, growth in EPS is calculated by reference to the annualised EPS for the period preceding. To calculate the growth rate for any single period, EPS figures must be available for two consecutive periods which are either:

- the previous reported period (historic)
- the last reported period (historic)
- the unreported period just ended (forecast)
- the current period not yet ended (forecast)
- the following period (forecast)

The calculation of earnings growth rate for a given period is as follows:

Step 1:

(EPS for period) - (previous EPS) = EPS change (+or-)

Step 2:

$$\frac{\textit{EPS change}}{\textit{previous EPS}} \times 100 = \textit{EPS growth (\%)}$$

(NOTE: A minus sign indicates negative growth. When necessary, EPS for individual periods are adjusted to an annualised basis before calculating growth.)

Calculating the growth rate on a rolling 12 months-ahead basis
To the extent that EPS forecasts are available, they will usually cover the next two unreported periods. Whenever possible, the growth figure shown

in the Key Statistics table is calculated on a rolling 12 months-ahead basis.

The 12 months ahead inevitably span two separate reporting periods. When forecasts are only available for the first of these, the growth rate for the first period is presumed to be valid for the second.

When the 12 months ahead span two separate periods and forecasts are available for both, the growth rate is averaged. To illustrate this, the following example shows the calculation of 12 months-ahead earnings growth for a hypothetical company, measured at 31st May 1994. Its next year end is 31st December 1994, and earnings forecasts are available for the current year to December 1994 and following year to December 1995.

	Year end 31 Dec 93 (Historic)	Year end 31 Dec 94 (Forecast)	Year end 31 Dec 95 Forecast)
EPS	15.7p	18.5p	21.0p
Giving annual growth of:	-	+17.8%	+13.5%
Apportionment:	-	7 months	5 months
Apportioned growth:	-	+10.4%	+5.6%

12 months-ahead growth rate
(1 Jun 94 to 31 May 95): . . . .+16.0%

(NOTE: A minus sign indicates negative growth. When necessary, EPS for individual periods are adjusted to an annualised basis before calculating growth.)

Use of 'normalised EPS'

In order to ensure that a reasonably realistic measure of growth is achieved, it is essential that comparison should only be made between EPS figures calculated on the same basis. This is particularly important when comparing historic EPS for consecutive periods, or when comparing the last reported EPS alongside a forecast for the following period.

To ensure comparability, any historic EPS figures used for measuring growth are calculated on a normalised basis which excludes any non-trading or exceptional profits and losses. This is because any forecast results almost certainly exclude the effect of such events. The full methodology for calculating normalised EPS is described on pages 144-9 under the heading: Calculation of IIMR Headline and normalised earnings.

Forecasts overtaken by preliminary results. When a preliminary result is announced, any existing consensus forecast for the next period is immediately rendered out of date, and must be treated with caution. Whilst revisions based on newly-available information are awaited from brokers, the existing consensus forecast may still be accepted as valid provided the previous forecast turned out to have been accurate. In this event, the growth rate is the percentage difference between the newly announced preliminary EPS (adjusted to a normalised basis) and the remaining unrevised consensus forecast for the following period.

However, when a preliminary announcement appears to render the existing consensus forecast invalid, it is not used at all. This rule is applied when the actual result for the current year differs from previous expectations by more than 5%.

N. PCF (PRICE-TO-CASH FLOW RATIO)

The calculation of PCF is as follows:

$$\frac{\textit{latest share price}}{\textit{cash flow per share}} = \textit{price-to-cash flow (x)}$$

Cash flow per share is calculated using information taken from the Cash Flow statement published in the latest available annual report. This is required to be published by companies in accordance with Financial Reporting Standard 1 (FRS1).

Cash flow can be regarded as the volume of cash, generated by the trading operations of the business, out of which the ordinary dividend must be funded.

A full description of the process for calculating cash flow per share is provided on page 141 and can be summarised as follows:

$$\frac{\textit{cash flow (£)}}{\textit{weighted average shares in issue}} \times 100p = \textit{cash flow per share (p)}$$

Cash flow per share can be subject to adjustment for a variety of reasons which fall into the following two categories:

- share capital changes which give rise to share price adjustment factors
- accounting periods which are greater or less than 12 months in duration

O. PSR (PRICE-TO-SALES RATIO)

The calculation of PSR is as follows:

$$\frac{\textit{latest share price}}{\textit{sales per share}} = \textit{PSR (x)}$$

Sales per share is calculated using information disclosed in the latest available annual report. It is the total sales or operating revenues for the period covered by the last annual report divided by the weighted average number of ordinary shares in issue during the period.

Total sales, or operating revenues, used in the calculation exclude any sales-based taxes, excise duty, government levies, or VAT, and are annualised when necessary.

The calculation of sales per share is as follows:

$$\frac{\textit{total sales}}{\textit{weighted average shares in isue}} \times \textit{100p} = \textit{sales per share(p)}$$

Sales per share can be subject to adjustment for a variety of reasons falling into the following two categories:

- share capital changes which give rise to share price adjustment factors
- accounting periods which are greater or less than 12 months in duration

P. PRR (PRICE-TO-RESEARCH & DEVELOPMENT RATIO)

The calculation of PRR is as follows:

$$\frac{\textit{latest share price}}{\textit{r \& d expenditure per share}} = \textit{PRR (x)}$$

(NOTE: The PRR is not shown if the result of the calculation is 100 or greater.)

Research and development ('r & d') expenditure per share is calculated using information disclosed in the latest available annual report, and is annualised where necessary. The r & d figure used is after deducting any amounts capitalised, and is divided by the weighted average number of ordinary shares in issue during the period.

The calculation of r & d per share is as follows:

$$\frac{\textit{r \& d expenditure (£)}}{\textit{weighted av. shares in issue}} \times \textit{100p} = \textit{r \& d per share (p)}$$

The r & d per share can be subject to adjustment for a variety of reasons falling into the following two categories:

- share capital changes which give rise to share price adjustment factors
- accounting periods which are greater or less than 12 months in duration

Q. PBV (PRICE-TO-BOOK VALUE)

The calculation of PBV is as follows:

$$\frac{\textit{latest share price}}{\textit{book value per share}} = \textit{PBV (x)}$$

Book value per share is calculated using information disclosed in the latest available annual report. The book value figure is divided by the weighted average number of ordinary shares in issue during the period.

The calculation of book value per share is as follows:

$$\frac{\textit{book value (£)}}{\textit{weighted av. shares in issue}} \times \textit{100p} = \textit{book value per share (p)}$$

Book value is calculated as follows:

  ordinary capital
\+ equity reserves
= book value (£)

The book value per share can be subject to adjustment for a variety of reasons, mostly reflecting share capital changes which give rise to share price adjustment factors.

R. *PTBV (PRICE-TO-TANGIBLE BOOK VALUE)*

The calculation of PTBV is as follows:

$$\frac{\textit{latest share price}}{\textit{tangible book value per share}} = \textit{PTBV (x)}$$

Tangible book value per share is calculated using information disclosed in the latest available annual report. The tangible book value figure is divided by the weighted average number of ordinary shares in issue during the period.

The calculation of tangible book value per share is as follows:

$$\frac{\textit{tangible book value (£)}}{\textit{weighted av. shares in issue}} \times 100p = \textit{tangible book value per share (p)}$$

Tangible book value is calculated as follows:

  ordinary capital
\+ equity reserves
\- intangible assets

= tangible book value (£)

Tangible book value per share can be subject to adjustment for a variety of reasons, mostly reflecting share capital changes which give rise to share price adjustment factors.

S. *GEAR (NET GEARING)*

Net gearing indicates overall indebtedness, and is measured relative to shareholders' funds at the last reported financial year-end (as disclosed in the latest available annual report). It is calculated by dividing net borrowings (i.e. gross borrowings less cash and near-cash assets) by shareholders' funds, and expressing the result as a percentage. For these calculations shareholders' funds *include* intangibles, and any preference capital redeemable within 12 months is classed as borrowings.

Near-cash assets

Near-cash assets are defined as current assets of a liquid nature which can readily be converted to cash, for example cash on overnight or short term deposit, treasury bills or CD's (Certificates of Deposit). Price sensitive items, such as marketable securities, are not included within near-cash assets.

Shareholders' funds

These are defined as follows:

  ordinary share capital
\+ preference share capital
\+ reserves

= shareholders' funds

Calculation:

$$\frac{\textit{total borrowings, less cash \& near-cash assets}}{\textit{shareholders' funds}} \times 100 = \textit{net gearing (\%)}$$

(NOTE: A minus sign indicates nil net gearing and denotes an overall net cash position.)

T. *MARGIN (TRADING MARGIN)*

This is the trading margin for the last reported period, showing trading profit as a percentage of sales, or total trading revenues.

The calculation is as follows:

$$\frac{\textit{trading profit}}{\textit{total sales (net of taxes)}} \times 100 = \textit{MARGIN (\%)}$$

Trading profit is taken to exclude any share of results of associated companies, and represents normalised pre-tax profit before crediting interest receivable and rental income, and before charging interest payable. As trading profit is based on normalised pre-tax profit, it also excludes all significant exceptional and non-trading elements of profit or loss, such as amounts written off intangibles or investments.

U. *ROCE (RETURN ON CAPITAL EMPLOYED)*

This measures the return achieved on invested and borrowed capital (the capital employed). The return is therefore taken to be the pre-tax profit earned before charging borrowing costs.

The calculation takes place as follows:

Step 1: calculate return

When calculating return, the starting point is taken as normalised pre-tax profit, which is the reported pre-tax profit after excluding any exceptional and non-trading items.

Thus:

pre-tax profit (normalised)
\+ interest paid
= return

(NOTE: In the event of the financial period being greater or less than twelve months in duration, the return is adjusted to an annualised basis.)

Step 2: calculate capital employed

The capital employed figure used in the ROCE calculation is after deducting any intangible assets, and consists of the following items from the last reported balance sheet:

ordinary capital
\+ reserves
\+ preference capital
\+ minority interests
\+ provisions
\+ total borrowings
\- intangibles
= Capital Employed

Step 3: calculate ROCE

The calculation is completed as follows:

$$\frac{\textit{return (annualised)}}{\textit{capital employed}} \times 100 = \textit{ROCE (\%)}$$

V. MARKET INDEX POSITION

The index ranking (e.g. FT-SE 100 - 16th) shows both the index within which the company is currently included, and its current position within that index after ranking all fellow constituents, including any Investment Trusts, according to their latest market capitalisation. Note that in all other respects Investment Trusts are outside the scope of *Company REFS* and do not therefore appear within the tables or as individual entries.

The following index designations are used:

FT-SE 100 Index
FT-SE Mid 250 Index
FT-SE SmallCap Index

Companies designated as 'USM' are traded on the Unlisted Securities Market.

Companies whose shares are temporarily suspended (e.g. pending an announcement) are ranked according to the last available share price. Companies suspended on an indefinite basis are removed from the rankings altogether. Suspended companies are recognised by an 'S' flag alongside the latest share price in the top right hand corner of the panel.

W. MARKET OVERALL POSITION

This shows the current position of the company within the market *overall* after ranking all fellow constituents, including any Investment Trusts, according to their latest market capitalisation. Note that in all other respects Investment Trusts are outside the scope of *Company REFS* and do not therefore appear within the tables or as individual entries.

Companies whose shares are temporarily suspended (e.g. pending an announcement) are ranked according to the last available share price. Companies suspended on an indefinite basis are removed from the rankings altogether. Suspended companies are recognised by an 'S' flag alongside the latest share price in the top right hand corner of the panel.

3

KEY DATES

This panel begins with the expected year-end date of the next annual report due to be published; this is normally the anniversary of the year-end of the last annual report received, unless a change is notified.

This is followed by a list of the key dates spanning the period since the year-end date of the last but one annual report received. The key dates refer to the nine most recent of the following events:

Previous reported year-end:

- ex-dividend dates with net amount declared (usually two per year)

Last reported year-end:

- ex-dividend dates with net amount declared (usually two per year)
- 1st quarter announcement date
- interim announcement date
- 3rd quarter announcement date
- year-end date
- preliminary announcement date
- last annual report posted date
- a.g.m. date

Next reported year-end:

- ex-dividend dates with net amount declared (usually two per year)
- 1st quarter announcement date
- interim announcement date
- 3rd quarter announcement date

A rule is drawn to indicate whether any of these events have yet to take place, for example a forthcoming a.g.m. date just announced, or the future ex-dividend date of a recently declared dividend.

(NOTE: If the last annual report is posted the same day as the annual results are announced, the preliminary announcement date is ignored.)

4

SECTOR AND ACTIVITIES ANALYSIS

A. SECTOR

The FT-SE Actuaries industry sector and sub-sector for each company which appears within *Company REFS* is found under the heading 'SECTOR'. The classification system is operated by the London Stock Exchange and the *Financial Times* in conjunction with the Institute and Faculty of Actuaries.

FT-SE Actuaries industry classification system

Every company is classified according to the industry sub-sector which most closely fits the business area from which the majority of its profits is earned. There are around 75 sub-sectors, which are grouped into 37 sectors belonging to the following six 'economic groups':

1. Mineral Extraction	*4. Services*
2. General Manufacturers	*5. Utilities*
3. Consumer Goods	*6. Financials*

For example, in the Mineral Extraction economic group there are three sectors and six sub-sectors, as follows:

SECTORS:	SUB-SECTORS:
Extractive Industries	Gold Mining Other Mineral Extractors & Mines Mining Finance
Oil, Integrated	Oil, Integrated
Oil Exploration and Production	Oil Exploration & Production Oil Services

Each sub-sector has a strict definition; Gold Mining, for example, is defined as 'Prospectors for, extractors and refiners of gold-bearing ores'.

The industry sub-sectors are defined to meet the requirements of the current FT-SE Actuaries industry classification system. This is used to allocate the constituent companies by size within the following share indices:

FT-SE 100
FT-SE Mid 250
FT-SE Actuaries 350
FT-SE SmallCap
FT-SE Actuaries All-Share

B. *ACTIVITIES ANALYSIS*

This panel analyses the proportions of turnover and profits directly attributable to the activities and regions indicated. The headings and figures are derived from the latest published annual report.

Presentation

The figures represent the company's own breakdown of turnover and profit, and are analysed by percentage. The headings are based on the descriptions used by the company and may be abbreviated for space reasons. No attempt has been made to standardise activity headings across all companies, nor the grouping of different geographical regions.

Use of headings

Similar companies can use markedly different bases for grouping both business segments and geographic areas. The Companies Act leaves the company a wide margin of discretion to define its own headings. It is equally unspecific as to the precise definition of turnover and profit. For example, the breakdown of profit given by a company, whether by region or by activity, can be shown at either operating or pre-tax profit level, and the definition of operating profit can itself vary between companies.

Limitations

The practical and legal requirements relating to company reporting allow companies a wide range of presentation options for turnover and profit analysis.

Whilst it would be possible to apply strict rules to ensure comparability, the practical effect would be to either exclude many companies from showing a breakdown within *Company REFS*, or to require the use of a table structure too complex to fit within the available space. A case-by-case approach has been adopted to provide a broad-brush indicator of how a company's main areas of product and regional activity inter-relate.

Definitions and analysis rules applied

A number of general rules and exceptions emphasise the practical, rather than precise, nature of the *Company REFS* activity analysis:

Origin of percentages
The upper and lower tables show percentages of the same turnover and profit figures. Percentages are rounded to the nearest whole number.

Space constraints
Space is provided for up to nine headings within the combined upper and lower tables; the smallest percentages are consolidated where necessary, with precedence in favour of turnover. To fit within the panel a company's own headings may need to be abbreviated or combined.

Business segment definitions
Descriptions used within *Company REFS* for business segments are based on each company's own headings and not on any uniform classification system. Heading definitions can vary from one company to another and two companies with the same range of activities can segment them differently. It should not be assumed that two companies which share the same segment descriptions within *Company REFS* are necessarily engaged in the same range of activities.

Geographical regions
Descriptions of geographical regions are based on each company's own headings, and are not uniform. The precise definition of regions can also vary from company to company. It is therefore possible for two companies with the same geographical spread of activities to group them under different headings. Likewise, two companies which share the same geographical headings within *Company REFS* do not necessarily operate within the same territories.

Definition of Turnover
Turnover is defined as invoiced sales net of sales-

based taxes, such as excise duty or VAT. Turnover can be analysed in two ways, namely by destination (i.e. where the goods are delivered to) or by origin (i.e. by location of subsidiary, or country of manufacture). Within *Company REFS* the turnover analysis is always by destination (when available).

Intra-group turnover
In consolidated or group accounts, it is normal for intra-group amounts to be excluded from the gross turnover figure, and for their activities or geographical breakdowns to be based on the net amount. However, where companies analyse the gross amount only, *Company REFS* follows suit.

Definition of profit
Wherever possible, the profit figure in activities analysis is the reported pre-tax profit. However, many companies analyse profit at the 'operating' level which is (usually) before interest and (sometimes) before related companies' profit share. *Company REFS* follows whichever basis the company uses.

Unallocated costs or income
When presenting their activities analysis, companies often analyse profit before deducting various unallocated costs (or before crediting unallocated income'). The analysis shown within *Company REFS* is based on whichever profit figure the company has elected to analyse.

Presentation of losses
Negative percentages refer to losses. Where there are both losses and profits, they are expressed as a percentage of either total profits or total losses, whichever is greater.

For example, if the net result is a profit, all profits add up to +100%, whilst individual losses are expressed as a negative percentage of total profits. Likewise if the net result is a loss, all losses add up to -100%, and individual profits are shown as a positive percentage of total losses.

The following examples illustrate a variety of situations where losses arise. The figures in bold would appear in the *Company REFS* activities analysis table.

Example 1

	£m		%
Industrial Plastics	(25)	-100	**-6**
Plastics Packaging	(30)		**-7**
Agricultural Products	(256)		**-59**
Heat Exchangers	(125)		**-28**
Net operating loss	(436)		

Example 2

	£m		%
Agricultural Products	256	100	**67**
Heat Exchangers	125		**33**
Industrial Plastics	(25)		**-7**
Plastics Packaging	(30)		**-8**
Net operating profit	326		

Example 3

	£m		%
Industrial Plastics	25	100	**8**
Plastics Packaging	30		**10**
Agricultural Products	256		**82**
Heat Exchangers	(125)		**-40**
Net operating profit	186		

Example 4

	£m		%
Industrial Plastics	(25)	-100	**-8**
Plastics Packaging	(30)		**-10**
Agricultural Products	(256)		**-82**
Heat Exchangers	125		**40**
Net operating loss	(186)		

Example 5

	£m	%
Agricultural Products	(256)	**-100**
Industrial Plastics	25	**10**
Plastics Packaging	30	**12**
Heat Exchangers	125	**49**
Net operating loss	(76)	

5

EARNINGS, DIVIDEND ESTIMATES

A. INTRODUCTION

This panel compares earnings and dividends per share for the last period reported with consensus brokers' estimates for the following two periods.

Source
The estimates are derived from fundamental research by stockbrokers' analysts. Research tends to relate either to companies which the brokers represent, or to stocks in which there is sufficient liquidity in the company's shares to justify the effort - in the expectation that business can be attracted. Some of the larger broking houses follow several hundred stocks. Others follow far fewer, and may perhaps concentrate on specific sectors. It follows that many stocks with low or negligible market turnover are not the focus of broker research.

Coverage
The approximate number of stocks for which estimates are available is no higher than 1,000, for the reasons explained in the preceding paragraph. Within *Company REFS* the criteria for inclusion apply to around 1,600 stocks, so about three entries out of eight do not include estimates. The words 'brokers do not prepare estimates for this company' are shown when this is the case.

Updating sequence
At the time of the preliminary announcement of a company's annual results, a shift occurs making the current year's forecast historic. When the suffix 'PA' appears, it signifies that the shift has taken place recently.

B. COLUMN HEADINGS

Column 1

The first column refers to the last reported period and is headed according to the appropriate calendar year; the suffix denotes the source, being either the Annual Report (AR), or a Preliminary Announcement (PA).

Columns 2 and 3

The second and third columns refer to the Estimates (suffix E) for the following two periods.

C. LINE HEADINGS

Norm EPS (Normalised earnings per share)

Normalised EPS are calculated as follows:

Step 1:

profit after tax
- minority interest
- preference dividends

= reported earnings (unadjusted)

Step 2:

reported earnings

\+ non-trading losses
\+ exceptional charges
\- non-trading profits
\- exceptional income

(*net of tax and minority interest adjustments*)

= normalised earnings

Step 3:

$$\frac{\textit{normalised earnings (£)}}{\textit{shares in issue}} \times 100p = \textit{norm EPS (p)}$$

Earnings are based on reported results in the first column, and estimated future results in the second and third columns. Reported earnings have been adjusted to normalised basis in order to achieve a more realistic comparison with future estimates.

For the first column, which shows the last reported EPS, the result is initially calculated by dividing the 'earnings' by the weighted average number of shares in issue during the year.

For the second and third columns, EPS is initially the result of dividing the consensus of brokers' forecast earnings by the current number of shares in issue. The consensus is taken as the average, or arithmetic mean, of all the individual contributing brokers' views, and the method of calculation is illustrated below under the heading: Calculation of consensus and standard deviation.

The figures for both earnings and the number of shares can be subject to adjustment for a variety of reasons which fall into the following four categories:

1. Non-trading and exceptional profits/losses

The forecast results almost certainly exclude the effect of any future exceptional or non-trading events. Because of this, the reported earnings are adjusted to a normalised basis. This provides a more realistic base from which EPS estimates for the following two periods can be compared, and forecast EPS growth can be measured. Normalised earnings are calculated by excluding any exceptional or non-trading profits and losses, and the methodology is fully explained on pages 144-9 under the heading: Calculation of IIMR Headline and normalised earnings.

2. Share capital changes.

If a change in share capital gives rise to a share price adjustment factor, the factor is applied to restore comparability between EPS figures from different time periods. Examples include rights issues, scrip issues, and share consolidations or subdivisions.

3. Annualisation

Adjustments are made to annualise the last reported EPS when the period is greater or less than 12 months in duration. Likewise the forecast EPS figures are presented on an annualised basis when the next expected reporting period is non-standard. The methodology is fully explained on page 151 under the heading: Annualisation.

4. Notional dilution

EPS is shown on a fully diluted basis. This notionally assumes that any known future possible share issues, which would take place upon conversion of other classes of debt or share capital, have already occurred. This involves applying adjustments to reflect, for example, lower preference dividend or interest payouts, or an increased earnings capacity through a larger capital base, as well as adjustments to the actual number of shares.

Change

Where a consensus EPS forecast for the relevant period existed one month previously, the change indicates in pence the amount by which the latest consensus has moved up (+) or down (-).

The calculation is as follows:

latest consensus EPS

– *consensus EPS 1 month ago*

= *change (p)*

Brokers

The number of stockbrokers or research houses whose individual estimates form the consensus forecast is indicated.

Std Dev (Standard deviation)

Standard deviation is a statistical measure of deviations from the mean known as the 'root mean square deviation'. The method of calculation is illustrated in the next two columns.

The standard deviation measures the degree to which individual numbers tend to spread about their average value. In *Company REFS* it indicates the amount by which individual estimates deviate from the overall consensus forecast. The lower the standard deviation in relation to the forecast EPS, the higher the degree of consensus between the contributing brokers.

The Standard Deviation is also useful for indicating the tightness of spread around the mean EPS (i.e. the consensus EPS). In statistical analysis, it is accepted that for a given sample of measurements, two-thirds normally fall within one Standard Deviation of the mean. For example, if there are 18 estimates, it can be assumed that 12 of them lie within plus or minus one Standard Deviation of the consensus.

Calculation of consensus and standard deviation

The following illustrations show, for a given company, how the consensus and standard deviation calculations are performed when applied to a range of broker forecasts of next year's earnings per share. A total of nine brokers are contributing to the consensus in the example, and the range of forecasts is as follows:

	Forecast EPS (p)
Broker 'A'	35.7
Broker 'B'	35.3
Broker 'C'	34.9
Broker 'D'	38.8
Broker 'E'	35.2
Broker 'F'	34.9
Broker 'G'	34.0
Broker 'H'	35.3
Broker 'I'	35.3

The consensus EPS is the arithmetic mean of all the forecasts, calculated as follows:

Step 1: Add the EPS forecasts in the consensus (319.4p).

Step 2: Count the number of brokers in the consensus (9).

Step 3: Divide the sum total of the EPS forecasts by the number of brokers to find the arithmetic mean, or consensus EPS (35.5p).

This can be summarised as follows:

$$\frac{\textit{Sum of the EPS forecasts}}{\textit{Number of brokers}} = \textit{consensus EPS (p)}$$

The calculation of standard deviation involves four steps to establish the root mean square of the deviations from the consensus, as follows:

Step 1: Calculate the deviation of each forecast from the consensus EPS

Step 2: Calculate the square of each deviation

Step 3: Find the mean of the squared deviations

Step 4: Calculate the square root of the mean to give the standard deviation

The following table illustrates how the standard deviation is derived from the data in the example:

Number of brokers: 9

Consensus EPS: 35.5p

	Forecast EPS (p)	Deviation from the consensus (p)	Square of each deviation (p)
Broker 'A'	35.7	+0.2	0.04
Broker 'B'	35.3	-0.2	0.04
Broker 'C'	34.9	-0.6	0.36
Broker 'D'	38.8	+3.3	10.89
Broker 'E'	35.2	-0.3	0.09
Broker 'F'	34.9	-0.6	0.36
Broker 'G'	34.0	-1.5	2.25
Broker 'H'	35.3	-0.2	0.04
Broker 'I'	35.3	-0.2	0.04

Total of the squares of each deviation = 4.11p

Mean of the squared deviations
(14.11 divided by 9) = 1.57p

Standard deviation
(square root of 1.57) = 1.25p

Growth

This line shows, for each period, how much EPS have grown, or are expected to grow, when measured against the previous period. A minus sign indicates negative growth. In order to ensure that the growth being measured reflects the trend of underlying earnings, reported EPS are compared on a normalised and annualised basis.

The growth shown in the left-hand column for the last reported period is calculated by reference to the previous year's normalised EPS. For the following two periods, it is the year-on-year percentage by which the normalised EPS must grow in order to achieve the consensus forecasts shown.

The calculation is as follows:

Step 1:

(this year's EPS)
– *(previous EPS)*

= *EPS change (+ or -)*

Step 2:

$$\frac{\textit{EPS change}}{\textit{previous EPS}} = \times 100 = \textit{EPS growth (\%)}$$

In order to ensure that a realistic measure of growth is achieved, it is essential that comparison should only be made between EPS figures calculated on a genuinely similar basis. This is particularly important when comparing historic EPS (based on reported results) for consecutive periods, or when comparing the last reported EPS with a forecast for the following period.

Historic EPS figures used for measuring growth are calculated on a normalised basis, which excludes any non-trading or exceptional profits and losses. This is because any forecast results almost certainly exclude the effect of any future events of that nature. The full methodology for calculating normalised EPS is described on pages 144-9 under the heading: Calculation of IIMR Headline and normalised earnings.

Where a preliminary results announcement has just been received, and brokers have not yet reacted, the growth percentage is based on comparing the newly announced historic normalised EPS for the latest period with the previously existing forecast for the following period. However, growth is not calculated when the actual result (i.e. the newly announced historic normalised EPS) deviates from the forecast it supersedes by more than 5%. Superseded estimates are explained in greater detail on pages 135-6.

PER (Price-earnings ratio)

The PER expresses the current share price as a multiple of the historic EPS for the last financial year, and as a multiple of the forecast EPS for the following two periods. The PERs are calculated using the latest price shown in the top right-hand corner of the entry.

The calculation is as follows:

Column 1:

$$PER = \frac{\textit{latest share price}}{\textit{normalised EPS (last reported)}}$$

Column 2:

$$PER = \frac{\textit{latest share price}}{\textit{consensus forecast EPS (results next due)}}$$

Column 3:

$$PER = \frac{\textit{latest share price}}{\textit{consensus forecast EPS (results after next)}}$$

DPS (Dividend per share)
For the first period shown, DPS is the total of the declared net dividend per share payable to registered ordinary shareholders in respect of the last period reported, adjusted where necessary to compensate for significant changes in year end or share capital.

For the following two periods shown, DPS is the consensus forecast dividend which is calculated by taking the average, or arithmetic mean, of all the individual brokers' forecasts of total net dividends per share for the period shown.

The figures for DPS can be subject to adjustment for a variety of reasons which fall into the following two categories:

1. Share capital changes.
If a change in share capital gives rise to a share price adjustment factor, the factor is applied to restore comparability between DPS figures from different time periods. Examples include rights issues, scrip issues, and share consolidations or subdivisions. When an adjustment arises between the interim and final dividends, the adjusted DPS combines the adjusted interim with the unadjusted final.

2. Annualisation
Adjustments are made to annualise the last reported DPS when the period is greater or less than 12 months in duration. Likewise, the forecast DPS figures are presented on an annualised basis when the next expected reporting period is non-standard. The methodology is fully explained on page 149 under the heading: Annualisation.

Div yield (Dividend yield)
The first column shows the historic dividend yield, which is the annualised gross dividend for the last reported period expressed as a percentage of the latest share price. The second and third columns show the prospective dividend yields, based on the latest share price and the consensus dividend forecasts for the following two periods.

The dividend yield expresses the annual dividend of a share as a percentage return on investment at its prevailing market price. The net dividend shown immediately above each dividend yield is grossed up by the appropriate rate of income tax and expressed as a percentage of the latest share price.

The calculation of dividend yield is performed as follows:

Step 1:

For the purpose of illustration, it is assumed that the standard income tax rate applicable to dividends which are declared net is 20%. On this basis, it follows that the net dividend per share is 80% of its gross value. The grossed-up dividend per share is therefore calculated as follows:

$$\textit{net dividend per share} \times \frac{100}{(100 - 20)} = \textit{gross dividend per share}$$

Step 2:

$$\frac{\textit{gross dividend per share}}{\textit{latest share price}} \times 100 = \textit{dividend yield (\%)}$$

D. SUPERSEDED ESTIMATES

The existing first year consensus forecast is immediately superseded upon the preliminary announcement of the actual results for the period. Pending the reaction of brokers in updating their individual forecasts, the existing second year consensus forecast may still be considered valid, however, provided the superseded first year forecast proves to have been reasonably accurate.

Forecasts are considered accurate if they are within 5% of the actual results achieved. If the superseded forecast is within this range limit the existing second year forecast is still held to be valid, and is used together with the newly announced normalised EPS to calculate growth.

If the superseded forecast fails this test of accuracy, the second year forecast can no longer be regarded as valid. In this event no forecasts are shown for earnings, dividend or growth until revised brokers' estimates are processsed, and the caption 'brokers are currently updating their estimates' appears temporarily within the table.

E. *PROFIT WARNINGS*

The market reaction to an unexpectedly adverse trading statement or profit warning issued by the company is usually immediate, and often has a profound impact on share price as reduced earnings expectations are digested. Profit warnings are closely followed by downwardly revised brokers' forecasts, and any existing brokers' forecasts shown in *Company REFS* are immediately rendered invalid pending the receipt of revised estimates which reflect the new information.

In this situation, no forecasts are shown for earnings, dividend or growth until revised broker estimates are processed. The caption 'brokers are currently updating their estimates' appears temporarily within the table.

6

HISTORICAL PERFORMANCE

A. INTRODUCTION

The Historical Performance panel measures the operating results of the last reported period in the context of the last five years' performance.

For each measure listed, the result of the last period is shown alongside the following comparatives:

- the average of the results of the last five reported periods
- the number of reversals within the last five reported periods
- the year-on-year trend measured over five full periods, and calculated using linear regression techniques

Number of periods
The number of comparable consecutive periods for which the average and trend can be calculated is sometimes less than five. This is indicated when a superscript is shown against the five-year average. The superscript indicates the number of periods to which the average and trend figures relate.

Source
Except for recently listed companies, the figures shown in the first column, and those used in calculating averages and trends, are derived from information published in annual reports. Where listing has occurred within the last five reporting periods, information is taken from the listing prospectus when necessary.

Restatement
Where an annual report shows comparative figures for the previous year which are different from those originally published, the restated figures are used.

Adjustment of figures
The per-share statistics shown for the last reported period, as well as those used in calculating averages and trends, are adjusted where necessary to compensate for:

- share capital changes which give rise to share price adjustment factors
- accounting periods which are greater or less than 12 months in duration

The rationale and mechanisms for applying these adjustments are explained on pages 149-51.

Dilution

Many companies have equity subscription rights in the form of warrants, or have classes of debt or fixed dividend capital which, at some future date, have rights of conversion or subscription into equity. These companies are required to publish information on earnings per share (EPS) which illustrates the potential dilution effect of conversion. Basic EPS can then be compared with EPS calculated on a 'fully diluted' basis.

In addition to any adjustments made within *Company REFS* to reflect actual share issues, all per-share figures are presented on a fully diluted basis when this produces a measurable difference.

B. COLUMN HEADINGS

Column 1: Derived from the last published annual report

The first column refers to the last reported period and is headed according to the appropriate calendar year; the suffix AR indicates that the source is the Annual Report.

Column 2: 5-Year Average

The second column shows the average value, or arithmetic mean, over the last five periods, annualised where necessary. Where there are less than five consecutive periods available, a superscript indicates the number of periods from which the average has been calculated.

Column 3: Reversals

The third column indicates the number of reversals within the series of results used to construct the average and trend values. A reversal is defined as a decreased result, or downturn, when compared with the immediately preceding period. An EPS reversal can arise through a reduction in EPS or an increase in losses per share.

Column 4: Trend

The fourth column displays the statistical trend of annual growth (+) or decline (-). This is the growth reflected by the series of results from which the average value shown in Column 2 is constructed, using an additional preceding base period where this is available.

The trend reflects the compound annual rate of growth derived by applying regression analysis techniques to interpolate a 'best-fit curve' plotted for *all* results in the series. It is *not* based solely on the opening and closing values in the series. A minimum of three values is required in order to calculate a growth trend.

Trend calculations - full technical definition

Equal weight is given to each value in the series, and no adjustments are made to favour recent performance. No distinction is made between a negative statistic with a reducing trend, and a positive statistic with an increasing trend.

The calculation method is described in three stages below. The description assumes the reader is familiar with the following statistical expressions:

- mean
- iteration
- correlation
- weighted average
- compound rate of growth
- discounted rate of growth
- coefficient of correlation
- least squares linear regression

Stage 1. Taking the series of values, the 'least-squares linear regression' is calculated, and then expressed as a percentage of the mean. The result is translated into a compound equivalent (Rate 1).

Stage 2. A process of iteration is used to establish a notional compound rate (Rate 2) which meets two conditions. Firstly, Rate 2 produces a notional data set which has the same linear regression as the original series of values. Secondly, if Rate 2 is used to discount the mean of the original series of values to the base date, the result is equal to the base value of the notional data set.

When the actual rate (Rate 1) is in fact a consistent year on year rate of change, the notional data set produced by Rate 2 matches the original series of values, and Rate 2 is identical to Rate 1.

Stage 3. The correlation coefficient of a) the original series of values to b) the notional data set (produced by Rate 2), is used to weight the average of Rates 1 and 2, which in turn gives the Trend result.

If the original series of values correlates perfectly with the notional data set (produced by Rate 2), then Rate 2 is the Trend result. If, on the other hand, the original series of values does not correlate at all with the notional data set, then Rate 1 is the Trend result.

If attempts to establish Rate 2 points to a base value of zero or below, (i.e. recovery from a negative position) or if Rate 1 reveals an adverse trend (i.e. a declining positive trend, or an increase in negative trend), the Trend result is taken to be Rate 1.

C. LINE HEADINGS

- **Norm EPS (Normalised earnings per share)**
- **IIMR EPS (IIMR Headline earnings per share)**
- **FRS3 EPS (FRS3 earnings per share)**

Adjustments
The figures for both earnings and number of shares can be subject to adjustment for a variety of reasons, including share capital changes, dilution, and non-standard periods. These are explained in detail at the end of this Section under the heading: Adjustments to figures, ratios & per share values.

Normalised earnings
Normalised earnings are calculated by taking reported results as a starting point, and then excluding any items which are exceptional, abnormal, or non-recurring in nature, together with any non-trading profits and losses.

IIMR Headline earnings
IIMR Headline earnings are calculated by taking reported results as a starting point, and then excluding any items which represent non-trading profits or losses. This adjustment is carried out in accordance with the current guidelines of the Institute of Investment Management and Research, the professional body of Investment Analysts and Fund Managers in the UK.

FRS3 earnings
FRS3 earnings are taken directly from the results as reported by the company under Financial Reporting Standard 3 (FRS3). FRS3 earnings reflect all items of profit or loss, including those which might be regarded as non-trading or exceptional in nature, and which might be considered to distort any view of underlying or maintainable performance.

Calculating FRS3, IIMR and normalised EPS
Earnings are initially based on reported results, and EPS are initially calculated by dividing the earnings for the year by the weighted average number of ordinary shares in issue during the year.

The process of calculating the three different measures of EPS is best seen as a three stage process, as follows:

Stage 1: FRS3 Earnings

(Calculate earnings as reported under FRS3)

	profit after tax	
-	minority interest	*as reported (unadjusted)*
-	preference dividends	
=	FRS3 earnings (£)	

$$\frac{\textit{FRS3 earnings (£)}}{\textit{weighted average shares in issue}} \times 100p = \textit{FRS3 EPS (p)}$$

Stage 2: IIMR Headline Earnings

(Adjust FRS3 earnings by applying the IIMR guidelines - see pages 144-9)

	FRS3 earnings	
+	non-trading losses	*net of tax and minority*
-	non-trading profits	*interest adjustments*
=	IIMR Headline earnings (£)	

$$\frac{\textit{IIMR Headline earnings (£)}}{\textit{weighted average shares in issue}} \times 100p = \textit{IIMR EPS (p)}$$

Stage 3: Normalised Earnings

(Exclude from IIMR Headline earnings any remaining significant exceptional trading profits and charges - see pages 144-9)

IIMR Headline earnings

+ exceptional charges | *net of tax and minority*
- exceptional income | *interest adjustments*

= normalised earnings (£)

$$\frac{\textit{normalised earnings (£)}}{\textit{weighted average shares in issue}} \times 100p = \textit{normalised EPS (p)}$$

Cflow ps (Cash flow per share)
Cash flow can be regarded as the volume of cash, generated by the trading operations of the business, out of which the ordinary dividend must be funded.

Cash flow is derived from the Cash Flow statement required by Financial Reporting Standard 1 (FRS1). The starting point for calculating cash flow in *Company REFS* is the figure appearing at the top of the published Cash Flow statement, namely the 'net cash inflow from operating activities'.

This, in turn, is based on the operating profit shown in the Profit & Loss account. It is adjusted, firstly, for items of revenue or cost which do not involve cash movement, such as depreciation or provisions and, secondly, for any non-operating cash flow which may arise, for example, when stocks and debtors are increased, or when creditors are reduced.

Interest actually received is then added, whilst interest, taxation, and preference dividends paid out are deducted. These adjustments are made in terms of cash receipts and payments; accruals and prepayments are eliminated. The share of associates' profits is restated in terms of dividends received, whilst the share of minority interests in profit is restated in terms of dividends paid out.

The resulting figure is the cash flow used in *Company REFS,* which is then divided by the weighted average number of ordinary shares in issue during the period to calculate cash flow per share.

The calculation of cash-flow can be summarised as follows:

Operating profit (as reported)

+ depreciation charges
+ asset write downs
+ net increase in provisions

- share of associates' profits (net)
- profits (net of losses) on asset disposals
- currency translation profits (net)

- net increase in stocks
- net increase in debtors
+ net increase in creditors

Net cash inflow from operating activities (as reported)

Add: Returns on investments

+ interest received
+ dividends received from associates
+ other investment receipts

Deduct: Servicing of finance (except dividends paid to ordinary shareholders)

- interest paid
- dividends paid to preference shareholders
- dividends paid to minority interests

Deduct: Taxation paid

= cash flow

The per share calculation is then made as follows:

$$\frac{\textit{cash flow (£)}}{\textit{weighted average shares in issue}} \times 100p = \textit{cash flow per share (p)}$$

The cash flow per share shown in Column 1, or used in calculating the figures for Columns 2-4, can be subject to adjustment for a variety of reasons falling into the following two categories:

- share capital changes which give rise to a share price adjustment factor
- accounting periods which are greater or less than 12 months in duration

(NOTE: FRS1 was introduced relatively recently, and applies to all financial periods ended 23rd March 1992 onwards. The average trend and reversal columns are based on post-FRS1 results only.)

Tax rate

The tax rate shows the effective overall rate of taxation provided against reported pre-tax profit (i.e. against the unadjusted FRS3 pre-tax profit). It therefore takes account not just of U.K. Corporation Tax, but of deferred tax, overseas taxation, double taxation relief, and any unrelieved ACT write-offs.

Prior year tax adjustments are not excluded from the total tax charge when calculating the overall tax rate; these relate to under- or over-provisions in previous years, and are regarded as being of a recurring nature whose effects cancelout over time.

Any share of results of associated companies is ignored for the purposes of this calculation, which is performed as follows:

Step 1:

Total tax charge (unadjusted FRS3)

\- Share of tax on results of Associated companies

= Tax charge excluding Associates

Step 2:

Pre-tax profit (unadjusted FRS3)

\- Share of pre-tax results of Associated companies

= Pre-tax profit excluding Associates

Step 3:

$$\frac{\textit{tax charge excl. Associates}}{\textit{pre-tax profits excl. Associates}} \times 100 = \textit{tax rate (\%)}$$

DPS (Dividend per share)

The DPS is the total of declared net dividends per share payable to registered ordinary shareholders in respect of the last period reported.

Individual dividends per share payable since the second last period end date are listed under Key Dates, space permitting, and refer to the actual unadjusted amount of net dividend declared at the time.

The DPS can be subject to adjustment for a variety of reasons falling into the following two categories:

- share capital changes which give rise to share price adjustment factors
- accounting periods which are greater or less than 12 months in duration

1. Share capital changes

The figures shown for DPS in Columns 1-4 are derived from a history of individual dividends declared during the past six financial periods. When a share capital change has taken place which results in a share price adjustment factor, the factor is applied to all previous dividends per share in the time series to restore comparability with subsequent dividends. This applies to rights issues, scrip issues, and share consolidations or subdivisions, and is explained in greater detail on pages 149-51 under the heading: Adjustments to figures, ratios & per share values.

2. Annualisation

Adjustments are made to annualise the last reported DPS where the financial period is greater or less than 12 months in duration. For the purposes of calculating the five-year average and trend, similar adjustments are applied, when necessary, to earlier periods.

Sales ps (Sales per share)

This shows total sales or operating revenues for the period covered by the last annual report, divided by the weighted average number of ordinary shares in issue during that period.

Total sales, or operating revenues, used in the calculation exclude any sales-based taxes, excise duty, government levies, or VAT, and are annualised when necessary.

The calculation is as follows:

$$\frac{\textit{total sales (£)}}{\textit{weighted average shares in issue}} \times 100p = \textit{sales per share (p)}$$

The sales per share shown in Column 1, or used in calculating the figures for Columns 2-4, can be subject to adjustment for a variety of reasons falling into the following two categories:

- share capital changes which give rise to share price adjustment factors
- accounting periods which are greater or less than 12 months in duration

Margin
This is the trading margin for the last period reported, showing trading profit as a percentage of sales, or total trading revenues.

The calculation is as follows:

$$\frac{\textit{trading profit}}{\textit{total sales (net of taxes)}} \times 100 = \textit{margin (\%)}$$

Trading profit excludes any share of results of associated companies, and represents normalised pre-tax profit before crediting interest receivable and rental income, and before charging interest payable. As trading profit is based on normalised pre-tax profit, it also excludes all significant exceptional and non-trading elements of profit or loss.

ROCE (Return on capital employed)
This measures the return achieved on invested and borrowed capital (the capital employed). The return is therefore taken to be the pre-tax profit earned before charging net borrowing costs.

When calculating ROCE, any intangible assets are deducted, i.e. the capital employed is taken to exclude intangibles.

ROCE is calculated as follows:

Step 1: Calculate return

When calculating return, the starting point is taken as the normalised pre-tax profit, which is the reported FRS3 pre-tax profit after excluding any exceptional and non-trading items. Thus:

pre-tax profit (normalised)
\+ interest paid

= return

(NOTE: In the event of the financial period being greater or less than 12 months in duration, the return is adjusted to an annualised basis.)

Step 2: Calculate capital employed

The capital employed figure used in the calculation consists of the following items from the last reported balance sheet:

ordinary capital
\+ reserves
\+ preference capital
\+ minority interests
\+ provisions
\+ total borrowings
\- intangibles

= capital employed

Step 3: Calculate ROCE

The calculation is completed as follows:

$$\frac{\textit{return (annualised)}}{\textit{capital employed}} \times 100 = \textit{ROCE (\%)}$$

D. *IMPACT OF FRS3 ON RESULTS OF EARLIER PERIODS*

When calculating the average and trend for EPS, margin or ROCE, and when determining the number of reversals, it is necessary to process a time series of reported results for up to six consecutive periods. It is essential to maintain comparability within each time series, so that a valid calculation can be obtained.

Given that FRS3 took effect in 1993, many companies reported for the first time under FRS3 relatively recently. With the benefit of restated comparatives published alongside the latest results, it is possible for *Company REFS* to make use of at least two comparable periods of results under FRS3, whilst in some cases there are more.

The comparability of pre-FRS3 periods is best examined on a line by line basis, since different assumptions may be relevant in each case.

(NOTE: The figures for cash flow per share, dividends per share, and sales per share are not affected by FRS3, and are not covered here.)

Norm EPS

The pre-FRS3 basis of calculating earnings per share tends to yield figures comparable with applying the normalisation process to post-FRS3 results. This is because the normalisation adjustments closely resemble the categories of item which, before the introduction of FRS3, would mostly have been labelled 'extraordinary'. For comparison purposes, therefore, Company REFS uses unmodified pre-FRS3 EPS alongside normalised post-FRS3 EPS figures, subject to adjustment for share capital changes or annualisation.

(NOTE: The average and trend calculations may be distorted where an unmodified pre-FRS3 EPS has been calculated after charging, or crediting, items labelled exceptional which, in a post-FRS3 situation, would be excluded from normalised EPS.)

IIMR EPS

It is not feasible to adjust pre-FRS3 results to a basis comparable with IIMR Headline EPS, and this is not attempted within *Company REFS*. Consequently, the average, trend and reversals columns are based on post-FRS3 results only.

FRS3 EPS

The most important distinction between FRS3 EPS, as reported now, and EPS reported for pre-FRS3 periods, is that the latter exclude extraordinary items. Unless provided by the company itself, however, FRS3 EPS cannot be accurately estimated, and whilst some companies have given summary FRS3 figures for earlier periods, others have not.

Tax rate

The tax rate shows the effective overall rate of taxation which the company provides against its reported pre-tax profit. It is based on the unadjusted pre-tax profit for both pre-FRS3 and post-FRS3 results. Therefore, tax rate figures for periods before and after FRS3 may not always be comparable.

Margin

For post-FRS3 results, margin is based on normalised pre-tax profit before interest which is adjusted back to a trading level.

The normalisation adjustments exclude any items which would have been labelled extraordinary before the introduction of FRS3. Therefore in *Company REFS* the normalised trading profit calculated for post-FRS3 results is considered comparable with the unmodified trading profit from pre-FRS3 results.

ROCE

For post-FRS3 results, return on capital employed is based on normalised pre-tax profit, adjusted to exclude the cost of borrowing.

In effect, the normalisation adjustments exclude any items which would have been labelled extraordinary before the introduction of FRS3. Therefore in *Company REFS* the normalised return calculated for post-FRS3 results is considered comparable with the unmodified return from pre-FRS3 results.

E. CALCULATION OF IIMR HEADLINE AND NORMALISED EARNINGS

The requirements of FRS3

For periods which end on, or after, 22nd June 1993, the annual accounts of companies are required to comply with Financial Reporting Standard 3 (FRS3). FRS3 takes the stance that no single earnings figure can be suitable for all purposes, and that readers of accounts should be encouraged to make their own profit adjustments so that the resulting earnings figure suits their particular need.

To achieve this, FRS3 requires that EPS reflect all Profit & Loss charges or credits, including those which are unusual, abnormal or non-recurring. Prior to FRS3 such items would mostly have been labelled 'extraordinary' and excluded from eps altogether.

To ensure that adjustments can be made properly, FRS3 requires Profit & Loss accounts to carry adequate descriptive information, and attributable tax and minority interest amounts, of any items which are, in reality, likely to be excluded from earnings calculations.

The purpose of adjusting earnings

In practice there are two principal reasons why analysts and others would wish to adjust a given historical recorded earnings figure. These are, firstly, to assess the level of currently maintainable performance in order to predict future results and, secondly, to assess underlying performance so that earnings growth can be measured.

Assessing maintainable performance.
Analysts tend to use the last recorded earnings as a basis for projecting the results of future periods. This requires making a forward-looking assessment of the level of maintainable performance, which forms the basis from which the future performance can be projected. For example, the results of discontinued activities can be excluded, whilst those of newly acquired businesses can be adjusted to cover a (theoretical) full 12 months.

The assessment of maintainable earnings, both past and future, involves a substantial amount of subjective judgement, and is not attempted within *Company REFS*. In this specialised field, analysts can use their expertise and judgement to produce earnings forecasts; *Company REFS* then incorporates these forecasts within a consensus estimate to calculate prospective statistics and indicators, such as growth.

Assessing underlying performance
For comparative purposes, analysts need to make a backward-looking assessment of the trend of underlying historical performance. Here it is desirable to exclude from earnings any items of an abnormal or unusual nature which would distort an underlying trend.

By contrast with maintainable earnings, underlying earnings can be more readily assessed on a consistent and objective basis. Two bases are used to present underlying earnings within *Company REFS*, IIMR Headline earnings and normalised earnings.

IIMR Headline earnings
IIMR Headline earnings are calculated in accordance with the Statement of Investment Practice issued by the Institute of Investment Management and Research (IIMR) in September 1993. The IIMR is the professional body representing investment analysts and fund managers within the UK. A copy of the full guidelines can be obtained for £15 from the Secretary General at the following address:

Institute of Investment Management and Research
211-213 High Street
Bromley
Kent BR1 1NY

Tel: 0181-464-0811

For IIMR purposes, the nature of each Profit & Loss item must be classified between trading on the one hand, and non-trading or capital on the other. The distinction between trading and non-trading items must be made regardless of size or significance, or whether they are abnormal or likely to recur.

Non-trading items can be defined as items of income or cost which can be separated from the FRS3 earnings figure on the basis that they are not of a trading nature.

Normalised earnings
In assessing a company's underlying earnings trend the crucial distinction for IIMR purposes is between trading items on the one hand, and non-trading or capital on the other. In reality the market tends additionally to discount items such as large redundancy costs, reorganisation costs, or an exceptional tax charge. These are each classed as being of a trading nature according to the IIMR guidelines, and therefore remain within the IIMR earnings figure.

In order to accommodate such items, *Company REFS* also shows figures based on normalised earnings. The paramount consideration for normalised purposes is the distorting effect on underlying earnings. For any item to qualify for adjustment in arriving at normalised earnings it must satisfy all of the following criteria:

1. The amount must be sufficiently large to have a materially distorting effect on the earnings per share trend.
2. Its nature must be separate from normal trading and clearly identifiable.
3. It must be unusual in nature and not expected to recur in the normal course of events.
4. It has been, or is likely to be, ignored by most analysts in establishing an actual earnings performance base upon which to build future estimates.

Within *Company REFS*, the normalised operating profit figure is used in the calculation of Margin and ROCE. The normalised EPS figure is used within the PER and PEG, and for measuring historic and forecast earnings growth.

Identifying IIMR and normalised earnings adjustments
The categories into which items tend to fall are listed below, together with how they are treated, ie. left *in* or taken *out* . The items taken *out* are therefore the IIMR and normalised adjustments respectively:

FRS3 earnings	IIMR earnings	Normalised earnings	
			Restructuring of the business:
IN	IN	OUT	Reorganisation and rationalisation costs relating to continuing activities
IN	IN	IN	Profits or losses from trading of operation(s) discontinued during the year
IN	OUT	OUT	Profits or losses on sale or termination of discontinued operation(s)
IN	OUT	OUT	Profits or losses on sale of business(es)
			Assets and investments:
IN	OUT	OUT	Profits or losses on sale of fixed assets not purchased for resale
IN	OUT	OUT	Amounts written off or diminution in value of fixed assets or business(es), not purchased for resale
IN	IN	IN	Profits, losses, write-offs or diminution in value of assets acquired for resale in the normal course of business
			Debt restructuring:
IN	OUT	OUT	Profits or losses on reorganisation or redemption of long-term debt
			Prior period adjustments:
IN	OUT	OUT	Prior period adjustments arising out of accounting policy changes
IN	OUT	OUT	Prior period adjustments arising out of past fundamental accounting errors
IN	IN	IN	Prior period adjustments of a normal, recurring nature (e.g. prior year tax adjustments within P & L tax charge) or adjustments to prior period accounting estimates
			Provisions:
IN	OUT	OUT	Provisions for future costs and losses (e.g. sale or termination of an operation to be discontinued in a subsequent year)
IN	OUT	OUT	Release of provision, made in prior years, for future costs and losses
IN	OUT	OUT	Utilisation or release of provision made in prior years for future costs and losses

FRS3 earnings	IIMR earnings	Normalised earnings	
			Goodwill:
IN	OUT	OUT	Goodwill depreciated through the Profit & Loss account
IN	OUT	OUT	Goodwill realised or written off on sale of business(es)
			Pension fund:
IN	IN	OUT	Exceptional pension fund costs or credits relating to continuing activities
IN	OUT	OUT	Pension fund costs relating to the discontinuation of an activity
IN	IN	OUT	Exceptional pension fund costs, provision, or credit transfer arising from: - bull or bear markets for equities - changes in actuarial assessments - conversion from defined benefit to defined contribution scheme
			Currency:
IN	IN	OUT	Exceptional currency effects on trading transactions
IN	OUT	OUT	Currency movements which change the valuation of long-term foreign assets or liabilities
			Tax charge:
IN	OUT	OUT	Tax charge(s) relating to items (as above) which are excluded from both IIMR and normalised earnings - see 'Adjusting for tax' (p. 148)
IN	IN	OUT	Tax charge(s) relating to items (as above) which are excluded from normalised, but not from IIMR earnings - see 'Adjusting for tax' (p. 148)
IN	IN	OUT	Exceptional taxation of an abnormal or non-recurring nature, other than prior period adjustments
			Minority interests:
IN	OUT	OUT	Minority interest(s) relating to items (as above) which are excluded from the IIMR headline earnings - see 'Adjusting for minority interest' (p. 148)
IN	IN	OUT	Minority interest(s) relating to items (as above) which are excluded from normalised, but not from IIMR earnings - see 'Adjusting for minority interest' (p. 148)
			Extraordinary items:
IN	OUT	OUT	Extraordinary items which, if they ever occur, must all now be included within FRS3 earnings

Adjusting for tax:

The element of corporation tax within the annual tax charge is based on the company's estimate of its taxable profit or loss, which is subject to assessment by the Inland Revenue. As with personal income tax, the assessment of taxable profit depends on which elements of income are taxable, and upon which items of expenditure are allowable for offset against this. It is not necessary to be concerned here with the detail of this calculation - merely the concept.

If any adjustments to the reported profit are needed in arriving at the IIMR or normalised earnings figures, it follows that in some instances it is necessary to make corresponding adjustments to the reported tax charge.

Once the earnings adjustments (ie. the items to be taken *out* of the reported FRS3 earnings) are identified, the next step is to establish whether any of the tax charge relates to those items. In most cases the company indicates the amount of tax attributable to the exceptional items shown under FRS3, although this may well be an aggregate figure.

Adjusting for minority interest

As with the tax charge, the minority interest charge shown under FRS3 may include an element which relates to exceptional items. If this is so, the company is required to show the amount involved.

It is likewise necessary to take any such amounts into consideration when adjusting reported FRS3 earnings to arrive at the IIMR and normalised earnings figures.

Calculating normalised and IIMR EPS

The process of adjusting to arrive at the IIMR and normalised earnings figures is illustrated using the following example, with exceptional items categorised as either trading or non-trading. The Profit & Loss statement might appear as in TABLE 1 (above right).

Calculating IIMR Headline earnings

In order to arrive at an IIMR earnings figure, it is necessary to reverse the effect of the non-trading exceptional items in the example. The full effects, from the operating profit level right down to retained profit, are demonstrated in TABLE 2 (right).

(NOTE: It has been assumed above that the adjustments do not have any minority interest implications.).

TABLE 1: Profit and Loss Statement

		£m
Turnover		835
Cost of sales		670
Net operating expenses		114
Operating profit before exceptionals		51
Exceptional profits (trading)		14
(Tax charge 4)		
Exceptional profits (non-trading)		7
(Tax charge 2)		
Exceptional charges (trading)		-3
(Tax credit 1)		
Exceptional charges (non-trading)		-1
(No Tax effect)		
Profit before interest		68
Net interest charged		18
Pretax profit		50
Tax charge before Exceptionals	14	
Tax charge on Exceptionals	5	
Tax charge		19
Profit after tax		31
Minority interest		2
Preference dividends		1
Available for ordinary shareholders		28
(FRS3 Earnings)		
Dividends		7
Retained profit		21

TABLE 2

	Reported Under FRS3	Add back: Exceptional. Charge (non-trading)	Subtract: Exceptional. Credit (non-trading)	IIMR Adjusted Figure
Profit before interest	68	1	(7)	62
Net interest	18	-	-	18
Pre-tax profit	50	1	(7)	44
Tax charge	19	-	(2)	17
Minority interest	2	-	-	2
Preference dividends	1	-	-	1
Earnings	28	1	(5)	24

TABLE 3	Reported Under FRS3	Add back: Exceptional Charge (trading)	Add back: Exceptional Charge (non-trading)	Subtract Exceptional Credit (trading)	Subtract: Exceptional Credit (non-trading)	Normalised Figure
Profit before interest	68	3	1	(14)	(7)	51
Net interest	18	-	-	-	-	18
Pre-tax profit	50	3	1	(14)	(7)	33
Tax charge	19	1	-	(4)	(2)	14
Minority interest	2	-	-	-	-	2
Preference dividends	1	-	-	-	-	1
Earnings	28	2	1	(10)	(5)	16

Calculating normalised earnings
Using the previous hypothetical example, let us assume that both of the trading exceptional items meet *all* the criteria applied in *Company REFS* for adjusting earnings to a normalised basis, and are therefore to be excluded. The effect is demonstrated in the TABLE 3 above.

F. ADJUSTMENTS TO FIGURES, RATIOS, & PER SHARE VALUES

Share capital changes

Introduction
When a significant share capital change occurs which gives rise to a share price adjustment, a mathematical correction is applied to any existing per share values, such as EPS or share prices, in order to maintain comparability with any values added subsequently.

A factor, or fraction, is applied retrospectively to any existing values when one of the following events occurs:

a) rights issue or open offer

b) scrip or capitalisation issue

c) share consolidation or subdivision

The key test as to whether a factor should apply in the event of a share capital change is simply whether the share price changes as a direct result of the event when it takes effect in the market, and the shares are first traded 'ex - event'.

When two or more events occur together, e.g. a subdivision of 25p shares into 5p followed immediately by a rights issue, then the individual factors calculated for each component are multiplied together.

Rights issues and open offers
Adjustment is made to reflect two separate elements. Firstly, the bonus element of the rights issue (or open offer) to existing shareholders, since this has a direct and measurable impact on share price. Secondly, the assumed increase in future earnings potential due to the enlarged capital base. An open offer is technically very similar to a rights issue, and the adjustment process is identical.

Scrip or capitalisation issues
Sometimes there are technical or practical reasons why a company may decide to increase the share capital in issue without actually raising any cash from shareholders. This can be achieved by capitalising some of its surplus reserves (a scrip or bonus issue) and increasing the number of shares in issue. The new shares created are then issued to existing shareholders on a pro-rata basis. Any previous per share values are adjusted by applying a correcting or compensating factor.

Share consolidations or subdivisions
Alternatively, the company may decide to

increase by subdivision or decrease by consolidation the number of shares in issue, without changing the combined value of the total share capital in issue. As with a scrip or bonus issue, it is necessary to apply a compensating factor to any previous per share values.

Calculation of adjustment factors

Rights issues and Open Offers
Formula for calculating a rights factor:

$$\frac{(\text{old shares} \times \text{cum rights price}) + (\text{new shares} \times \text{issue price})}{(\text{old shares} + \text{new shares}) \times \text{cum rights price}}$$

Example of rights issue details:

Issue of 2 new shares for every 5 already held (a 2 for 5 rights issue)

- Issue price - 255p
- Ex-rights date - 19th April
- Last cum rights price on 18th April - 325p

Calculating a rights factor for the above example:

$$\frac{(5 \times 325) + (2 \times 255p)}{(5 + 2) \times 325p} = \frac{1625 + 510}{7 \times 325} = \frac{2135}{2275} = 0.938$$

Applying the rights factor:

If, for example, the dividend per share for the previous period was 15.5p, and the rights issue above occurred after the year-end, the rights factor of 0.938 would be applied to give the following adjusted dividend per share:

$$15.5p \times 0.938 = 14.5p$$

Scrip issues
Formula for calculating a scrip factor:

Where 'old shares' is the number of shares in issue beforehand, and 'new shares' is the number of shares in issue afterwards, the factor is simply:

$$\frac{\text{old shares}}{\text{new shares}}$$

Example of scrip issue details:

A company decides to capitalise £x million of reserves by way of a bonus issue of 2 new ordinary shares of 25p nominal value for every 3 existing shares held (a 2 for 3 scrip issue). In other words after the bonus issue any shareholders who previously held, for example, 3,000 shares of 25p each would now hold a new total of 5,000 shares of 25p.

Calculating a scrip factor for the above example:

$$\frac{\text{old shares}}{\text{new shares}} = \frac{3}{5} = 0.6$$

Share consolidations or subdivisions
Formula for calculating the adjustment factor:

Where 'old shares' is the number of shares in issue beforehand, and 'new shares' is the number of shares in issue afterwards, the factor is simply:

$$\frac{\text{old shares}}{\text{new shares}}$$

Example of share consolidation details:

A company decides to halve the number of shares in issue from 10 million to 5 million by consolidating every 2 existing shares of 25p nominal value into 1 new share of 50p nominal value (a 2 into 1 consolidation). The total nominal value of the issued share capital remains unchanged at £2.5 million. After the consolidation any shareholders who previously held, for example, 3,000 shares of 25p each now have a new total of 1,500 shares of 50p each. Whilst the share price will probably have doubled, all other things being equal, they now have only half as many shares as before, so the overall value of their holding remains the same.

Calculating an adjustment factor for the above consolidation:

$$\frac{\text{old shares}}{\text{new shares}} = \frac{1}{3} = 0.333$$

Example of share subdivision details:

A company decides to treble the number of shares in issue from 10 million to 30 million by subdividing each existing share of 30p nominal value into 3 new shares of 10p nominal value (a 1 into 3 subdivision). The total nominal value of the issued share capital remains unchanged at £12 million. After the subdivision any shareholders who previously held, for example, 1,000 shares of 30p each now hold a new total of 3,000 shares of 10p each. Whilst the share price will probably have fallen by two thirds, all other things being equal, they now have three times as many shares as before, so the overall value of their holding remains the same.

Calculating an adjustment factor for the above subdivision:

$$\frac{\textit{old shares}}{\textit{new shares}} = \frac{1}{3} = 0.333$$

Annualisation

Introduction
If a company changes its financial year end, for example from 31st December to 31st March, then its next annual accounts will cover a reporting period of either 3 months or 15 months, rather than the regular 12 months. In this situation,many of the statistics in *Company REFS* for the non-standard period are adjusted to compensate, and are shown on a per annum basis rather than as reported.

Examples of figures which would need to be adjusted to an annualised basis, or would be affected by such adjustments, include EPS, growth, annual DPS, PER, ROCE, and PCF. Note that this is not an exhaustive list.

Examples of figures which would *not* need to be annualised include gearing, margin, tax rate, and interest cover.

Illustration
Below is an illustration of how the inclusion of a non-standard period can distort a trend, and how the distortion can be corrected by adjustment to a per annum basis:

A company regularly increases sales by 20% each year. Having last reported to 31st December 1991, it decides that its next accounts will cover the 15 months to 31st March 1993. The sales figures would appear on an as reported basis as follows:

Period End	31 Dec 1990	31 Dec 1991	31 Mar 1993	31 Mar 1994
Duration	12m	12m	15m	12m
Sales (£m)	1,200	1,440	2,160	2,074

The annual increase in sales, without compensating for the change in year end, would appear as follows:

Period End	31 Dec 1990	31 Dec 1991	31 Mar 1993	31 Mar 1994
Increase	+20%	+20%	+50%	-4%

To adjust the sales figures to an annualised basis, the sales for the non-standard period are divided by the number of days in that period (456 days in the example), and then multiplied by 365.

$$2,160 \times \frac{365}{456} = 1,729$$

Thus the sales for the 15 months to 31st March 1993 are adjusted as follows:
The sales figures now appear on an annualised, or per annum, basis as follows:

Period End	31 Dec 1990	31 Dec 1991	31 Mar 1993	31 Mar 1994
Duration	12m	12m	15m	12m
Sales (£m)	1,200	1,440	1,729 p.a.	2,074

The annual increase in sales, after compensating for the change in year end, is now in line with expectations as follows:

Period End	31 Dec 1990	31 Dec 1991	31 Mar 1993	31 Mar 1994
Increase	+20%	+20%	+20%	+20%

Notional dilution

If the future conversion of other classes of share capital or debt causes a potential dilution of earnings when measured on a per share basis, *Company REFS* shows historic EPS on a comparable, fully diluted, basis.

Any statistic or calculation which incorporates, or invites comparison with, historic EPS is also presented on a fully diluted basis.

Those affected include:

- historic and forecast EPS
- historic and forecast earnings growth
- historic cash flow per share
- prospective PER
- PEG

Full dilution notionally assumes that any known future possible share issues, which would take place upon conversion of other classes of debt or share capital, have already occurred. This involves applying adjustments to reflect, for example, lower dividend or interest payouts, or an increased earnings capacity through a larger capital base, as well as to the actual number of shares.

7

SHARE PRICE GRAPH AND OUTLOOK

A. INTRODUCTION

The share price graph and its surrounding area shows a range of information which can be summarised under the following headings:

- Scale factor, defining the vertical intervals on the log scale
- Adjusted share price plot
- Adjusted EPS plot
- Relative strength plot
- Share class and denomination
- Annual high and low prices
- Average annual historic PER
- Relative percentage movements of price vs. FT-SE Actuaries All-Share Index
- Beta relative, indicating the company's share price volatility relative to the FT-SE Actuaries All-Share Index
- Trading outlook statements abstracted from the latest annual report and subsequent announcements

B. *VERTICAL SCALE*

Selection of vertical scale extremes
The three arrays of data represented on the graph are the share price and relative strength plotted at each month-end, and the rebased normalised EPS (actual or forecast) plotted at each financial year-end.

The extremes of the vertical share price scale are chosen so that the scale can accommodate the highest and lowest share price and relative strength, and the highest EPS. With the exception, therefore, of the lowest EPS values, the three arrays of data are then scanned in order to establish the highest and lowest values which arise over the timescale for which they are to be plotted. This is a maximum of seven calendar years, with historic prices for up to five years past and broker forecasts for up to two years ahead.

Selecting the scale factor.
The scale factor expresses the height ratio of the vertical share price scale, and this in turn is the ratio of the upper extreme of the scale to the lower extreme. For example a scale ranging from 200p down to 50p has a height ratio of 4:1, which is equivalent to a scale factor of 4.

The scale factor is selected so that in the first instance the graph scale can accommodate the highest and lowest values to be plotted. The scale factor is then increased (i.e. the scale is then compressed) to a value of at least four (or a higher value if necessary e.g. 8, 16, 32, 64, 128) to ensure that the maximum number of graphs can be directly compared with others in *Company REFS*. If, for example, a share price fluctuated between 100p and 150p, it would be represented on a graph with a vertical scale from 100p to 400p in the same way as a share whose price moved between 100p and 390p.

Logarithmic scale, or 'Log scale'
The use of a log scale offers several statistical and interpretational advantages over a linear scale. It is employed for two principal reasons:

Firstly, it measures vertical movement on a proportional basis; this ensures that a given percentage movement is always represented by the same distance on the vertical scale. If, for example, a share price doubles from 40p to 80p, the vertical movement is exactly the same if it doubles again to 160p.

Secondly, it allows direct comparison to be made between any graphs in *Company REFS* which share a common vertical scale. Thus a graph with a scale ranging from 240p down to 60p is comparable with another ranging from 720p down to 180p. In both cases the highest price is four times the lowest, implying a height ratio of 4:1, a scale factor of 4.

A single common scale accommodating all companies is not used because it would need to encompass extremes of, say, £25 down to 1p. This would severely restrict the amount of vertical movement which most of the graphs could display, greatly diminishing the visual impact of all but a few graphs.

Company REFS therefore employs Scale 4 as a standard log scale in around 70% of the graphs whilst, for the remainder, the log scale is compressed to accommodate the full range of movement required.

When Scale 4 is insufficient to accommodate the extremes of movement, it is multiplied to the next appropriate higher value (e.g. Scale 8, Scale 16, Scale 32, etc.), and the value is shown above the graph.

Examples:
A share price with a 5-year high of 399p and a low of 173p would fit comfortably on a standard Scale 4 graph. 399p divided by 173p is less than 4.

A share with a range of 132p to 596p, however, would require a Scale 8 graph. 596p divided by 132p is greater than 4 but less than 8.

Scale factor
Above the upper right corner of the graph, space is reserved for a legend to display the scale factor (for example, Scale 8, or Scale 16). The scale factor defines the degree of vertical compression applied to the vertical log scale, as explained above under the heading 'Logarithmic scale'. The scale factor is only printed if it is greater than the default value, which is Scale 4. From a purely statistical standpoint, any two graphs which share a common scale factor can be directly compared if they are superimposed, even if the two scales have different price ranges.

C. *ADJUSTED SHARE PRICE PLOT*

The share price is shown over five calendar years, including the current year, as a solid line. This line is shaded underneath for visual emphasis.

It is smoothed by averaging prices on a monthly basis. However, the annual high and low prices displayed below the graph are based on daily prices, and may therefore show a range greater than the plot itself indicates.

D. ADJUSTED EPS PLOT

This plot represents historic normalised EPS and is extended into the future using brokers' forecasts, where these are available. It consists of a series of small circles, representing rebased EPS on the vertical scale, and accounting year-end dates on the horizontal scale; the circles are joined by theoretical straight lines, which refer to historic EPS when solid and forecast EPS when broken.

The process of getting the EPS plot to fit onto the same scale as the share price is called 'rebasing', and is separately explained under its own heading below.

The extension of the plot into the future is based on the consensus of brokers' forecasts of the company's future EPS.

Provided that two specific conditions are met, the forward extension of the EPS plot should reflect in which direction and at what rate the share price might be expected to move. These conditions are, firstly, that the current price-earnings ratio does not change and, secondly, that current brokers' forecasts are borne out by actual future results.

Rebasing of the EPS plot.

Rebasing involves three separate actions:

First, a point is chosen where the EPS plot can intersect the share price plot; along the horizontal axis, this is normally the date of the latest share price plotted and, on the vertical axis, the actual price on that date.

Second, a factor is determined which, when multiplied by the latest EPS value at the chosen date, gives the share price at the intended intersection point. This is actually the price-earnings ratio at that point in time.

Third, the rebasing factor is applied to each EPS value. The rebased EPS series is then plotted against the vertical share price scale, using small circles joined by a theoretical straight line.

The point of intersection chosen for the EPS plot is always, against the vertical scale, a closing share price. Against the horizontal scale, it can be one of three points, chosen as follows:

1. Latest share price on the graph.
   This is the usual point chosen, and requires two conditions to be met. First, that the EPS plot extends into the future, in other words that it reflects brokers' consensus forecasts. Second, that the last reported and next expected EPS values are both positive (i.e. there must be positive EPS values falling immediately either side of the intersection point, namely the latest share price).

2. Share price on the year-end date for which the last preliminary results were announced.
   This point of intersection is chosen as the first default when the last two reported results are both positive but there are no brokers' forecasts available to extend the EPS plot into the future.

3. Earliest share price on the graph.
   This intersection point is chosen as the second default, and applies when recent losses preclude the use of the options described above.

Presentation of low and negative EPS values

In order to fix the upper and lower extremes of the share price scale, the lowest EPS value is ignored. As a result, low and negative EPS values may be rendered out of range, and no attempt is made to plot these within the graph.

When the EPS plot is required to join values lying within the graph with those which lie beyond the bottom range of the scale, the outlying values are notionally plotted against the same scale extended downwards, and the angle of inclination of the plot itself is thus established. For low EPS values which are positive, the steepness of inclination reflects the rate of decline or growth between values lying within and beyond the graph. For EPS values which are negative, the angle of inclination can be almost vertical.

E. RELATIVE STRENGTH PLOT

The relative strength plot shows how the share price has moved relative to the market, as represented by the FT-SE Actuaries All-Share Index. This is commmonly referred to as 'price relative' performance. It is the broken line which floats within and outside the shaded area, and which is superimposed and rebased so that it starts from the same point as the share price plot.

A rise in the relative strength plot indicates outperformance, a fall shows underperformance. For example, if the relative strength plot doubles in value by reference to the vertical scale, the shares have outperformed the index by a factor of two. A horizontal line indicates that the share price has precisely tracked the Index.

The relative strength plot is determined by applying to a constant (the value of the index on the date the plot commences) a time series of factors which comprise the adjusted share price as the numerator and the index as the denominator.

Interpretation of the relative strength plot

Share prices, and the value of the companies they reflect, are expected to grow over the long term. A share price plot (the solid line) will therefore normally rise. But how can you tell how well one company compares with others? One way is to look at several graphs together, but there are physical and practical problems - especially if they are on different pages of the same book, as with *Company REFS*.

The relative strength plot (the broken line) provides a benchmark. It shows at a glance how well a share price has performed relative to the market as a whole, and is ideally rising - to show outperformance. When the plot is horizontal, the share has performed in line with the market index, neither better nor worse.

When the relative strength plot crosses the same horizontal level at different dates, it indicates a matching of the index between those dates. Rises and falls between the dates indicate short term out- or underperformance.

As well as giving a general visual indication, the relative strength plot also shows in precise terms, by reference to the vertical scale, how much better or worse than the market index the share price performance has been.

Assume, for example, that the relative strength plot rises by 50% when measured against the vertical scale (e.g. from 300 to 450). Without needing to examine either the share price or the index values, this shows that the share price has, in relative terms, performed 50% better than the market index over the same period.

This is not to say that the share price has necessarily risen by 50%, or indeed that it has risen at all. In fact the share price may well have fallen; but it will only have fallen by half as much as the index. Conversely, if the share price has risen, it will have risen in relative terms by 50% more than the index.

In *Company REFS* the relative strength plot is rebased so that it starts from the same point as the share price plot. This is done for two reasons: first, to provide a comfortable visual reference point and, second, to make the most of the height available without having to compress the vertical scale.

It is important to appreciate that the two individual plots (i.e. share price and relative strength) are shown together solely to make efficient use of space. In most respects (apart from the coincidental sharing of common scales) *each plot should be interpreted separately.*

Common characteristics of the relative strength plot

The relative strength plot tends to show a number of common characteristics.

Historically, markets have continued to rise in line with the momentum of global economic growth. As the market rises, the price of the average share also tends to rise over the long term. If the share price of this average share faithfully tracks the rising movement of the market, then its relative strength plot remains absolutely horizontal. In a rising market, therefore, share price plots should show an upward trend, with relative strength plots tending towards the horizontal. In most cases, under average market conditions, the relative strength plot (the broken line) tends to run beneath the share price plot (solid line).

However, when conditions take a downturn, these effects are reversed for the duration of a falling market. This is visible in the graph when the share price plot descends more quickly (or rises more slowly) than the relative strength plot. Over a longer period of market depression, the relative strength plot of the average company tends to run above the share price plot.

This can be illustrated by visualising a company whose share price moves perfectly in line with the market. For such a company, the relative strength plot is a perfectly horizontal flat line. In a rising market, the share price plot for that company is going up all the time, i.e. rising above the horizontal relative strength plot. In a falling market, the opposite will occur, and the share price plot for that company is going down all the time, ie. falling below the horizontal relative strength plot.

In a market which is completely flat, for any given individual share price trend, the relative strength plot tracks it precisely. If the share price goes up, the relative strength plot rises with it; if the price plot moves downwards, the relative strength movement is identical.

In practice, the normal pattern lies somewhere between these extremes. The market tends to be rising, and therefore both the price plot and its relative strength follow an upward trend, with the price plot rising slightly faster. The rate of change for the price itself is greater than its rate of change relative to the market as a whole.

F. *SHARE CLASS & DENOMINATION*

The legend above the middle of the graph shows the share class to which all the data relates, e.g. '25p Ords', the index used to calculate relative performance (the FT-SE Actuaries All-Share Index) and the earnings measure used for the EPS plot. To the left is the currency denomination, usually 'p' for pence.

G. *ANNUAL HIGH & LOW ADJUSTED SHARE PRICES*

The annual high and low share prices displayed below the graph are based on daily prices, whereas the graph itself is based on monthly averages. The highs and lows may, therefore, range beyond the values indicated by the graph. When a share capital change gives rise to an adjustment factor, the previous high and low share price values are adjusted retrospectively.

H. *AVERAGE PER*

The average price-earnings ratio (PER) at the foot of the graph is the average of all month-end PERs calculated during each year shown. The month-end PERs are the result of dividing, at each month-end, the prevailing share price by the prevailing historic normalised EPS.

I. *RELATIVE %*

This shows how the Company's adjusted share price has performed in percentage terms relative to the FT-SE Actuaries All-Share Index. This is commonly referred to as 'relative strength'. The figures show percentage outperformance (+) or underperformance (-) over the past month, three months, twelve months and two years.

Relative strength is calculated as follows:

$$\text{Price Change} = \frac{\text{Current Share Price}}{\text{Initial Share Price (adj)}}$$

$$\text{Index Change} = \frac{\text{Current Index Value}}{\text{Initial Index Value}}$$

Price movement relative to index (%) =

$$\frac{[\text{Price Change} - \text{Index Change}]}{\text{Index Change}} \times 100$$

The following five examples show how this works in practice:

Price Examples:

	Initial Value	Current Value	Change
1.	200	40	-80%
2.	200	160	-20%
3.	200	400	+100%
4.	200	240	+20%
5.	200	200	nil

Index Examples:

	Initial Value	Current Value	Change
1.	1,000	1,000	nil
2.	1,000	1,200	+20%
3.	1,000	2,000	+100%
4.	1,000	800	-20%
5.	1,000	200	-80%

Relative Strength (i.e. price movement relative to index) :

Example 1.

Price	-80%
Index	unchanged
Relative Strength	-80%

Example 2

Price	-20%
Index	+20%
Relative Strength	-33%

Example 3.

Price	+100%
Index	+100%
Relative Strength	+0%

Example 4.

Price	+20%
Index	-20%
Relative Strength	+50%

Example 5.

Price	unchanged
Index	-80%
Relative Strength	+400%

J. BETA RELATIVE

The beta relative measures the volatility of the share price relative to the volatility of the market as a whole. The movement of the market as a whole can be represented by an index, and for *Company REFS* the FT-SE Actuaries All-Share Index is used.

Examples:

Beta relative of 1.50 - the share price is 1.5 times more volatile than the market index. This is the case if the company's share price consistently follows the same direction as the market index, but on average moves by 50% more than the index.

Beta relative of 0.75 - the share price is 0.75 times as volatile as the market index. This is the case if the company's share price consistently follows the same direction as the market index, but on average moves by 25% less than the index.

Beta relative of 1.00 - the share price is exactly as volatile as the market index. This is the case if the company's share price consistently follows the same direction as the market index, and on average moves by exactly the same percentage as the index.

Note that share price movement does not always follow the same direction as the market index, whereas the examples illustrate shares which do, and which move by a constant rate relative to the index. In real-life, the average effect over time could well be similar, and it is this overall picture which the beta relative illustrates. The beta relative measures the average amount, over time, by which the share price moves more, or less, than the index.

A share with a beta relative of 1.00 moves, on average, exactly the same relative amount as the index.

Measurement requirements of the beta relative

When calculating a beta relative, both the measurement interval (e.g. daily) and the elapsed time covered (e.g. one week) can be varied to suit the prevailing requirements. Once chosen, they must then be consistently applied to allow valid comparisons to be made.

In *Company REFS*, the measurement interval is monthly, and the elapsed time covered is two years.

Calculating the beta relative

The beta relative of a given share is calculated by measuring the volatility of the share price relative to the volatility of the portfolio it belongs to. In *Company REFS* this is the notional market portfolio represented by the FT-SE Actuaries All-Share Index.

To illustrate the calculation, the table opposite relates to observations at regular month-end intervals of the FT-SE Actuaries All-Share Index and the share price of Marks & Spencer PLC over a two year period (during 1992 and 1993).

Starting with the first four columns, the table shows at each month-end the value of the FT-SE Actuaries All-Share index in column 'a', the index return (i.e. the percentage change in the index) in column 'b', the M&S share price in column 'c', and the share price return

Beta relative calculation - data used in the example:

	Column a	Column b	Column c	Column d	Column e	Column f	Column g	Column h
month	FT-SE A	% a	M & S	% c	variance		covariance	
end	All-Sh	+ or -	price	+ or -	b - x	d - y	e × f	e × e
12/91	1187.70	-	278.5	-	-	-	-	-
1/92	1227.84	3.38	298.0	7.00	1.82	4.78	8.70	3.31
2/92	1229.84	0.16	322.0	8.05	-1.40	5.83	-8.16	1.96
3/92	1171.71	-4.73	291.0	-9.63	-6.29	-11.85	74.54	39.56
4/92	1282.75	9.48	340.0	16.84	7.92	14.62	115.79	62.73
5/92	1311.79	2.26	341.0	0.29	0.70	-1.93	-1.35	0.49
6/92	1216.62	-7.25	331.0	-2.93	-8.81	-5.15	45.37	77.62
7/92	1143.14	-6.04	308.5	-6.80	-7.60	-9.02	68.55	57.76
8/92	1096.99	-4.04	295.0	-4.38	-5.60	-6.60	36.96	31.36
9/92	1206.16	9.95	325.5	10.34	8.39	8.12	68.13	70.39
10/92	1256.67	4.19	322.0	-1.08	2.63	-3.30	-8.68	6.92
11/92	1313.02	4.48	332.5	3.26	2.92	1.04	3.04	8.53
12/92	1363.79	3.87	329.5	-0.90	2.31	-3.12	-7.21	5.34
1/93	1364.33	0.04	314.0	-4.70	-1.52	-6.92	10.52	2.31
2/93	1396.53	2.36	330.0	5.10	0.80	2.88	2.30	0.64
3/93	1408.07	0.83	338.0	2.42	-0.73	0.20	-0.15	0.53
4/93	1388.88	-1.36	345.5	2.22	-2.92	-	-	8.53
5/93	1403.42	1.05	332.5	-3.76	-0.51	-5.98	3.05	0.26
6/93	1432.31	2.06	347.0	4.36	0.50	2.14	1.07	0.25
7/93	1448.76	1.15	353.0	1.73	-0.41	-0.49	0.20	0.17
8/93	1537.21	6.11	377.0	6.80	4.55	4.58	20.84	20.70
9/93	1506.55	-1.99	387.5	2.79	-3.55	0.57	-2.02	12.60
10/93	1565.37	3.90	403.5	4.13	2.34	1.91	4.47	5.48
11/93	1556.45	-0.57	431.0	6.82	-2.13	4.60	-9.80	4.54
12/93	1682.14	8.08	453.5	5.22	6.52	3.00	19.56	42.51
Total:		**37.37**		**53.19**			**445.72**	**464.49**
Average:		**+1.56**		**+2.22**			**+18.57**	**+19.35**
		(x)		**(y)**				

for M&S in column 'd'. The mean, or average, values for columns 'b' and 'd' appear at the bottom as 'x' and 'y' respectively.

The beta relative calculation is performed as follows:

Step 1: Calculate the monthly index variance. This appears in column 'e', and is the index return 'b' for each month minus the average index return 'x' over the two year period of +1.56.

Step 2: Calculate the monthly M&S variance. This appears in column 'f', and is the M&S return 'd' for each month minus the average M&S return 'y' over the two year period of +2.22.

Step 3: Calculate the covariance between the M&S share price and the index. This appears in column 'g', and is the index variance 'e' at each monthly interval multiplied by the M&S variance 'f'. The average covariance of +18.57 is given at the foot of the column.

Step 4: Calculate the covariance of the index with itself. This appears in column 'h', and is the index variance 'e' for each interval multiplied by itself. The average covariance of +19.35 appears at the bottom.

Step 5: The beta relative is calculated by comparing the average covariance between the M&S share price and the index (+18.57), to the average covariance of the index with itself (+19.35), as follows:

$$\textit{Beta relative} = \frac{+\,18.57}{+\,19.35} = +0.96$$

K. OUTLOOK

The text of any statement (e.g. the Chairman's review) provided by the company within the last annual report, and within any subsequent statements (e.g. trading statement, or interim or preliminary announcement), is scanned to abstract any remarks *which allude to the company's trading prospects.*

Each outlook statement is preceded by the date and source. '(8-Jun-94) Prelim: ch', for example, indicates remarks by the chairman from the preliminary results announcement dated 8th June 1994. In the absence of any such remarks, the words 'no outlook statement' appear instead.

Outlook statements are shown in chronological order, and are retained until superseded by the latest annual report. Space constraints dictate that outlook statements are sometimes abbreviated, and may consist of two or more elements separated by '...', where appropriate.

8

SHARE CAPITAL, HOLDINGS, DEALINGS

A. INTRODUCTION

This panel gives a breakdown of share capital, showing for each class the current number in issue, and the aggregate percentage held by major shareholders and directors respectively.

For the main equity class in issue, the current holdings of major shareholders and directors are also listed in detail, with indicators to highlight the timing and nature of the most recent dealings within the past six months.

Space is available for a maximum of ten lines, which is sufficient in most cases. If this is not enough, priority is given to share capital, and then (in most instances) to up to four major shareholders and five directors.

B. SHARE CAPITAL

Each class of share is listed, showing the current number of shares in issue (e.g. 124m) and a description (e.g. 25p Ords). All classes are shown, including preference shares, warrants and convertibles. The main class of equity share is listed first.

The total percentage held by major shareholders and by directors is noted after each class of share, unless this is less than 0.01%. The notation '[d]' follows when any director has dealt in the shares during the preceding six months.

The total percentage held by major shareholders includes:

- the holdings of each major shareholder, whether corporate or personal
- large non-beneficial holdings (i.e. more than 3.00%) of individual directors, for example held through directorships of large corporate shareholders, or through employee pension funds

(NOTE: Directors' non-beneficial holdings below 3.00% are not shown.)

The total percentage held by directors includes:

- the beneficial holdings of each director (aggregated with any family holdings)
- the beneficial holdings of any director who is also a major shareholder (i.e. with a beneficial holding of more than 3.00%)

C. LISTING OF MAJOR SHAREHOLDERS

Major shareholders are listed in order of size for the first share class shown. If an increased or decreased holding has been reported within the past six months, an indicator (e.g. '5+') is shown alongside the percentage holding. Interpretation of this indicator is covered below under the heading 'Last significant dealing transaction'.

The list of major shareholders includes, under the name of the actual beneficial holder, any large holding (i.e. more than 3.00%) declared as non-beneficial by a director.

(NOTE: Any beneficial directors' holdings are listed as such, regardless of size.)

D. LISTING OF DIRECTORS' HOLDINGS

Space permitting, the list of directors' holdings includes all notifiable beneficial holdings in the first share class shown. Directors' beneficial holdings of more than 3.00% appear as directors' holdings, and not as major shareholders.

Directors' holdings can be shown as either the number of shares held or, as with major shareholders, as a percentage. If a director has reported an increased or decreased holding within the past six months, an indicator (e.g. '5+') is shown alongside the number or percentage held showing the nature and timing of the last transaction.

Full details of the last transaction, together with any others which have occurred within the past six months, are provided separately in the schedule of Directors' Share Dealings which is found in the companion Tables Volume.

(NOTE: Dealings of less than £2,500 in value are ignored, as are 'bed & breakfast' deals and shares issued in lieu of dividends.)

Directors and their holdings are selected and listed according to the following hierarchy:

1. Executive Chairman (ch)
2. Managing Director (md) or Chief Executive (ce)
3. Finance Director (fd)
4. Non-executive Chairman *(ch)
5. Executive Directors (in annual report order)
6. Non-executive Directors (in annual report order)

A non-executive chairman or director is identified with an asterisk. Titles are abbreviated as above, and qualified by the following prefixes: vice (v), deputy (d), group (g), and joint (j). Dual roles are linked with '&', e.g. chairman and joint managing director (ch & jmd).

Other abbreviated titles include:

President (p)

Company Secretary (cs)

Chief Executive Officer (ceo)

Chief Operating Officer (coo)

Sales (s)

Marketing (mkt)

The size of shareholding is indicated as follows:

under 1,000	........n	number of shares
1,000 or more	.......k	thousands of shares
1,000,000 or more (up to 1.00%)	. . .m	millions of shares
1.00% or more	......%	percentage of shares in issue

The listing of directors' holdings includes beneficial holdings only. Directors' non-beneficial holdings are shown only where they are large (i.e. more than 3.00%), and appear not as directors' holdings but as major shareholders under the name of the actual beneficial holder.

E. LAST SIGNIFICANT DEALING TRANSACTION

If a major shareholder or director has reported an increased or decreased holding within the past six months, an indicator (e.g. '5+') is shown alongside the number of shares or percentage held. The indicators show the following information for the most recently recorded deal.

The number shows how many months ago the last reported deal occurred. The suffix shows the outcome of the deal. If, for example, the current month (as printed on the front cover) is December:

1- indicates that a decrease occurred during the previous month (i.e. November)

5+ shows an increase occurred 5 months ago (i.e. during July)

5N. indicates that a newly declared holding was reported 5 months ago (in July)

(NOTE: For a major shareholder who is not a director, individual dealing transactions need be notified to the Stock Exchange only when they cause the resultant holding to change to a new 0.5% band. This rule does not apply to directors' dealings, which must all be notified.)

9

GEARING, COVER

A. INTRODUCTION.

This panel provides an insight into:

- Balance Sheet structure
- levels of gearing
- the effect of intangibles on the gearing figure
- the relationship between invested and borrowed capital
- the cash position and short-term liquidity
- the extent of cover for interest and dividends payable

B. ABBREVIATIONS AND USE OF SYMBOLS.

Gearing calculations.
Gearing is not calculated for banks and insurance companies, and the abbreviation 'na' means 'not applicable'. For other companies, a dash ('-') indicates that gearing is nil. The abbreviation 'neg' indicates that negative shareholders' funds preclude the calculation of gearing.

Quick ratio, current ratio, interest and dividend cover
For banks and insurance companies, the quick

ratio and current ratio do not apply, and the abbreviation 'na' appears. For other companies 'na' would indicate, for example, that the interest charge or dividend payout is nil, and the corresponding cover ratios are not applicable. When the interest charge or dividend payout is low or negligible, and the calculation of cover returns a very high value, the abbreviation 'vhi' appears. A minus sign appears when interest cover or dividend cover is negative.

C. MEASURES OF GEARING

The analysis of borrowings is taken from the last available Balance Sheet as published by the Company in its latest Annual Report. The panel heading indicates the source (i.e. AR - Annual Report) and the relevant date (e.g. 93 - 1993 year end) which can be read from the accompanying 'Key Dates' panel.

Intangible assets in the context of Gearing
In general, the Gearing figures within *Company REFS* are calculated by dividing borrowings over different periods of maturity by shareholders' funds, and expressing the result as a percentage. However, the gearing figure itself provides an incomplete picture if the effect of intangible assets is ignored. In order to ensure that the impact of any intangibles is shown, *Company REFS* provides two gearing figures alongside each of the headings in the table.

The left-hand column shows each variable expressed as a percentage of shareholders' funds including intangibles, i.e. before deducting intangible assets. The right-hand column shows the same variable, but expressed as a percentage of shareholders' funds excluding intangibles, i.e. after deducting intangible assets.

Gearing is not calculated where shareholders' funds are negative, and this condition is indicated by the abbreviation 'neg'.

D. DEFINITION OF BALANCE SHEET VARIABLES

Intangibles
Intangible assets include goodwill, brand names, patents or publishing titles. They possess the following attributes:

- non-physical in nature
- capable of producing a future economic benefit
- protected by a legally recognised, or de facto, right
- capable of being separately identified
- capable of being objectively valued

The categories of intangible asset most frequently observed are:

- Purchased goodwill (i.e. the difference between the price paid for a business and the values attributable to its underlying tangible assets)
- Brands (e.g. product brand names, trademarks, corporate names, consumer goods brands)
- Publishing rights (e.g. magazine titles, books, newspaper mastheads, film rights, music rights)
- Intellectual property (e.g. patents, copyrights, technology, software, knowhow)
- Licences (e.g. TV and radio licences, airline take-off and landing slots, franchises, distribution rights)

Shareholders' funds - including intangibles
These are defined as follows:

ordinary share capital
\+ preference share capital
\+ reserves

Shareholders' funds - excluding intangibles
These are defined as follows:

ordinary share capital
\+ preference share capital
\+ reserves
\- intangible assets

(NOTE: For the purpose of gearing calculations, any preference capital redeemable within 12 months is classed as borrowings.)

E. GEARING CALCULATIONS

Net gearing
Net gearing is calculated by dividing net bor-

rowings (i.e. gross borrowings less cash and near-cash assets) by shareholders' funds, and expressing the result as a percentage. Near-cash assets are defined below under the heading 'Cash'.

Calculation:

$$\frac{\textit{total borrowings, less cash \& near-cash assets}}{\textit{shareholders' funds}} \times 100 = \textit{net gearing (\%)}$$

Separate figures are calculated to show net gearing both before and after deducting intangibles from shareholders' funds. A minus sign indicates nil net gearing and denotes a net cash position.

Cash
This shows the proportion of total cash and near-cash assets to shareholders' funds.

Near-cash assets are defined as current assets of a liquid nature which can readily be converted to cash, for example cash on overnight or short-term deposit, treasury bills or CD's (Certificates of Deposit).

Price sensitive items, such as marketable securities, are not included within near-cash assets for two reasons. Firstly, the market price itself can fluctuate, and the balance sheet valuation may no longer apply. Secondly, securities may or may not be marketable at the actual market price. A company's liquid cash position should arguably be assessed with this risk factor removed.

Calculation:

$$\frac{\textit{cash + near-cash assets}}{\textit{shareholders' funds}} \times 100 = \textit{cash (\%)}$$

To enable the impact of intangible assets to be considered when assessing the company's cash position, the cash percentage is calculated both before and after deducting intangibles from shareholders' funds.

Gross gearing
Gross gearing is calculated by dividing total gross borrowings by shareholders' funds, and expressing the result as a percentage.

Cash and other near-cash assets are not deducted from gross borrowings, but their significance can be separately assessed by reference to the cash percentage shown immediately above.

Calculation:

$$\frac{\textit{total borrowings}}{\textit{shareholders' funds}} \times 100 = \textit{gross gearing (\%)}$$

Separate figures are calculated to show gross gearing both before and after deducting intangibles from shareholders' funds.

Gearing under 5 Years
This shows the proportion of total medium and short-term borrowings to shareholders' funds. Medium-term borrowings are defined as loans and other debt due for repayment between one and five years' hence. Short-term borrowings refer to debt repayable on demand or within one year. Cash and other liquid assets are not deducted.

Calculation:

$$\frac{\textit{debt due within 5yrs}}{\textit{shareholders' funds}} \times 100 = \textit{gearing under 5 yrs (\%)}$$

Separate figures are calculated to show gearing under 5 years both before and after deducting intangibles from shareholders' funds.

Gearing under 1 year
This shows the proportion of total short-term borrowings to shareholders' funds. Short-term borrowings refers to debt repayable on demand or within one year. Cash and other liquid assets are not deducted.

Calculation:

$$\frac{\textit{debt due within 1 yr}}{\textit{shareholders' funds}} \times 100 = \textit{gearing under 1 yr (\%)}$$

Separate figures are calculated to show gearing under 1 year both before and after deducting intangibles from shareholders' funds.

F. MEASURES OF COVER

Quick ratio
This expresses a company's ability to repay short-term creditors, or current liabilities, out of its most liquid assets. The quick ratio is the result of dividing quick assets, the total of current assets other than stocks and work in progress, by current liabilities. It shows the number of times current liabilities are covered by quick assets. A value greater than 1.00 indicates positive cover. For banks and insurance companies, the quick ratio does not apply, and the abbreviation 'na' appears.

Calculation:

$$\frac{\textit{total current assets, less Stocks \& WIP}}{\textit{current liabilities}} = \textit{quick ratio (r)}$$

Current ratio
This reflects a company's current liquidity position, indicating its ability to meet current liabilities, or short-term creditors, out of current assets. The current ratio is the result of dividing the current assets total by current liabilities, and shows the number of times current liabilities are covered by current assets. A value greater than 1.00 indicates positive cover. For banks and insurance companies, the current ratio does not apply, and the abbreviation 'na' appears.

Calculation:

$$\frac{\textit{current assets}}{\textit{current liabilities}} = \textit{current ratio (r)}$$

Interest cover
This expresses a company's ability to pay interest on borrowings out of profits earned. It is calculated by taking the figure for normalised pre-tax profit, adding back gross interest, and dividing the result by gross interest.

The abbreviation 'na' indicates that the interest charge is nil, and interest cover is not applicable. When the interest charge is low or negligible, and the calculation of cover returns a very high value, the abbreviation 'vhi' appears. A minus sign appears when normalised profit before interest and tax is negative.

Calculation:

$$\frac{\textit{normalised pre-tax profit} + \textit{gross interest}}{\textit{gross interest charge}} = \textit{interest cover (x)}$$

Dividend cover
This expresses a company's ability to pay dividends to ordinary shareholders out of profits earned. It is calculated by taking normalised earnings and dividing by ordinary dividends payable.

The abbreviation 'na' indicates that the dividend payout is nil, and dividend cover is not applicable. When the dividend payout is low or negligible, and the calculation of cover returns a very high value, the abbreviation 'vhi' appears. A minus sign appears when normalised earnings attributable to ordinary shareholders are negative.

Calculation:

$$\frac{\textit{normalised earnings}}{\textit{ordinary dividends payable}} = \textit{dividend cover (x)}$$

INDEX

H

I

Q

R

S

FOLD OUT FOR KEY TO
COMPANY REFS ENTRY

Key to Company Entry

Non-standard scale factor (4 = standard)

Plot of actual share price

Plot of share price movements relative to the All-Share Index

— normalised eps
---- brokers' consensus forecast
o denotes the financial period end

Percentage share price movements in relation to the All-Share Index

Beta rel = volatility of the share price in relation to the All-Share Index (1 = the index)

Abstracts of statements by the company regarding its future outlook.

NB = Additional explanation regarding alert flag in the key statistics section

± change = increase/decrease in the consensus compared with a month ago

E = based on brokers' consensus estimates

brokers = number of brokers contributing to the consensus

std dev = standard deviation indicating the diversity of forecasts encompassed within the consensus

growth = the percentage growth that the latest results and each consensus estimate represent over the preceding year

per = price-earnings ratio based on current price and indicated eps

dps = historic and forecast dividend per share

div yield = historic and forecast gross dividend yield based on current price and indicated dps

Sector and subsector according to the Institute of Actuaries industry classification system

Analysis by activity and region, showing:

T/0 = turnover as a percentage of total turnover

Pr = profit as a percentage of total profit

NMS = normal market-size

Date of latest share price

Share price at close of business on date indicated

Major event-flag
T = involvement in takeover
S = suspended
R = forthcoming rights issue

(pr) prospective based on apportionment of brokers' forecasts for the next 12 months

94 AR = based on 1994 annual report figures (PA indicates preliminary announcement)

Denotes non-standard period (in months)

Gauges indicate ranking value of data relative to other companies in market (m) or sector (s)

EXAMPLE COMPANY

PRICE (p) 25p Ords vs FT-SE All-Share vs norm eps (Scale 8)

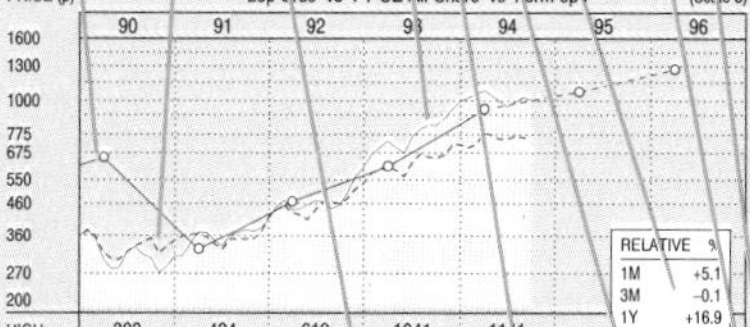

	90	91	92	93	94	95	96
HIGH	393	424	619	1041	1141		
LOW	246	302	417	614	910		
AVE PER	9.9x	20.2x	21.6x	26.7x	23.9x		

Price scale: 1600, 1300, 1000, 775, 675, 550, 460, 360, 270, 200

RELATIVE	%
1M	+5.1
3M	-0.1
1Y	+16.9
2Y	+65.2
Beta rel	0.93

ACTIVITIES: Development, manufacture and sale of specialised products and services for the healthcare sector. **TEL:** (0171) 278 7769 **REGISTRAR:** Barkers, Leeds. Tel: (01966) 473926 **BROKERS:** Bullish Securities
OUTLOOK: (13 Jun-94) AR: ch - "All our subsidiaries are now trading profitably. I am confident that you will share in the even greater success of your company in the year to March 1995".
NB: Recommended £87m takeover offer made for Smaller Group PLC.

SECTOR
Health care.

ACTIVITIES ANALYSIS (94AR)

		T/C	Pr
Clinical laboratories	%	44	59
Healthcare services	%	35	17
Environmental services	%	13	12
Medical equipment	%	5	12
Other activities	%	3	-5
Europe	%	41	72
North America	%	46	20
Asia/Pacific	%	13	8

EARNINGS, DIVIDEND ESTIMATES

		94AR	95E	96E
norm eps	p	47.6	54.4	64.6
change	p		–	+0.40
brokers	n		16	16
std dev	p		2.05	5.29
growth	%	52.0	14.3	18.8
per	x	20.7	18.1	15.2
dps	p	15.5	17.9	20.7
div yield	%	1.97	2.28	2.63

PRICE (NMS 5) 26-SEP-94 **985p** [T]

norm eps (pr)	59.5p
market cap	£314m
turnover (94AR)^{9}	£298m
pretax (94AR)	£42.4m

			m	s
DY (pr)	%	2.45		
PER (pr)	x	16.7		
PEG (pr)	f	1.00		
GR (pr)	%	16.5		
PCF	x	15.0		
PSR	x	1.00		
PRR	x	26.5		
PBV	x	4.16		
PTBV	x	4.26		
GEAR	%	−1.77		
MARGIN	%	13.6		
ROCE	%	21.9		

FT-SE Mid 250	192nd
market overall	292th

SHARE CAPITAL, HOLDINGS, DEALINGS

31.9m 25p Ords (Maj 28.8%, Dirs 2.04% [d]).

National Pens Tstee Co	%	6.23	
HS Staff Superan'tn Fd	%	3.67	
Monument Group	%	3.15	
Sloane Asset Management	%	15.7	
D I Barlow (ce)	k	175	2+
D S Watt (fd)	k	3.00	
Sir Philip Marlowe CBE * (ch)	k	5.00	
J Rockford	%	1.45	2+
Dr R Kimble OBE	k	6.50	

GEARING, COVER (94AR)

intangibles		Incl	Excl
net gearing	%	−1.77	−1.89
cash	%	37.6	38.5
gross gearing	%	35.8	36.6
under 5 yrs	%	35.8	36.6
under 1 yr	%	4.16	4.27
quick ratio	r		2.11
current ratio	r		2.56
interest cover	x		22.9
dividend cover	x		3.70

HISTORICAL PERFORMANCE

		94AR	5Y-av	Y↓	Tr%
norm eps	p	47.6	30.3	1↓	+11.3
IIMR eps	p	47.6	34.0^{3}		+42.9
FRS3 eps	p	48.0	33.6^{3}		+42.0
cflow ps	p	65.6	56.2^{4}	1↓	+9.18
tax rate	%	34.8	32.7	2↓	-3.02
dps	p	15.5	12.9		+6.62
sales ps	£	9.84	9.12	1↓	+9.23
margin	%	13.6	10.6	2↓	−3.92
ROCE	%	21.9	16.7	2↓	+0.64

KEY DATES

next AR year end	31-Mar-95
int xd (3.90p)	9-Nov-92
fin xd (9.60p)	14-Jun-93
int results	3-Nov-93
int xd (4.30p)	8-Nov-93
year end	31-Mar-94
prelim results	31-May-94
annual report	14-Jun-94
fin xd (11.2p)	14-Jun-94
agm	8-Jul-94

DY = dividend yield (gross)

PER = price-earnings ratio

PEG = price-earnings growth factor

GR = eps growth rate for the next 12 months based on consensus of brokers' forecasts

PCF = price-to-cash flow ratio

PSR = price-to-sales ratio

PRR = price-to-R&D expenditure ratio

PBV = price-to-book value including intangibles

PTBV = price-to-tangible book value

GEAR = net gearing - net borrowings as a percentage of share capital and reserves (including intangibles). Negative indicates net cash.

MARGIN = profit margin - pretax profit (excluding exceptional items, net interest and investment income) as a percentage of turnover

ROCE = return on capital employed (excluding intangibles)

Position in index and the market overall ranked by market capitalisation, indicating potential promotion and demotion candidates

[d] indicates that directors' dealings have taken place within the preceding 6 months

Unit denominating size of holding
n = number of shares
k = thousands of shares
m = millions of shares (up to 1%)
% = percentage of shares in issue

± denotes the timing and nature of the last reported change in holding within the last six months. In this case 2+ means that two months ago the holding was increased

net and gross borrowings and cash expressed as a percentage of share capital and reserves including and excluding intangibles

norm eps = earnings per share normalised to exclude exceptional items

IIMR eps = eps calculated in accordance with the guidelines set down by the Institute of Investment Management and Research

FRS3 eps = company reported eps

cflow ps = cash flow per share

5Y-av = average over the last five years.

Indicates the number of years included in the average and trend, if less than five.

Y↓ = number of downturns (compared with the preceding year) during the last five years.

Tr% = percentage per annum increase/decrease trend established using linear regression techniques

Dates of company reports, accounting periods and shareholders meetings

ex dividend date and net dividend declared (not adjusted for subsequent rights or scrip issues)